8
WAYS
to
GREAT

G. P. Putnam's Sons

New York

8

WAYS

to

GREAT

—

PEAK PERFORMANCE ON THE JOB AND IN YOUR LIFE

DR. DOUG HIRSCHHORN

PUTNAM

G. P. PUTNAM'S SONS
Publishers Since 1838
Published by the Penguin Group
Penguin Group (USA) Inc., 375 Hudson Street, New York, New York 10014,
USA • Penguin Group (Canada), 90 Eglinton Avenue East, Suite 700,
Toronto, Ontario M4P 2Y3, Canada (a division of Pearson Penguin Canada
Inc.) • Penguin Books Ltd, 80 Strand, London WC2R 0RL, England •
Penguin Ireland, 25 St Stephen's Green, Dublin 2, Ireland
(a division of Penguin Books Ltd) • Penguin Group (Australia),
250 Camberwell Road, Camberwell, Victoria 3124, Australia
(a division of Pearson Australia Group Pty Ltd) •
Penguin Books India Pvt Ltd, 11 Community Centre, Panchsheel Park,
New Delhi–110 017, India • Penguin Group (NZ), 67 Apollo Drive, Rosedale,
North Shore 0632, New Zealand (a division of Pearson New Zealand Ltd)
• Penguin Books (South Africa) (Pty) Ltd, 24 Sturdee Avenue, Rosebank,
Johannesburg 2196, South Africa

Penguin Books Ltd, Registered Offices:
80 Strand, London WC2R 0RL, England

Library of Congress Cataloging-in-Publication Data

Hirschhorn, Doug.
8 ways to great: peak performance on the job and in your life /
Doug Hirschhorn.
p.   cm.
ISBN 978-0-399-15608-3
1. Success in business.   2. Employees—Coaching of.   I. Title.
II. Title: 8 ways to great.
HF5386.H617   2010   2009023797
658.3'124—dc22

Printed in the United States of America
1   3   5   7   9   10   8   6   4   2

BOOK DESIGN BY AMANDA DEWEY

C.H.A.M.P.® is a registered trademark of Douglas K. Hirschhorn.

Dr. Doug Hirschhorn's expertise is in the psychology of achieving peak
performance. Dr. Doug Hirschhorn is not a financial adviser and does not make
trading or investment recommendations or provide trading or investment advice.
He is an expert on the mental game. Although Doug Hirschhorn has a Ph.D. in
psychology with a specialization in sport psychology, he is not a licensed
psychologist and does not provide therapeutic, clinical, or counseling services.

While the author has made every effort to provide accurate telephone numbers
and Internet addresses at the time of publication, neither the publisher nor the
author assumes any responsibility for errors, or for changes that occur after
publication. Further, the publisher does not have any control over and does not
assume any responsibility for author or third-party websites or their content.

To my wife, Amy.

CONTENTS

———

8
WAYS
to
GREAT

Why the 8 Principles Are Going to Help *You*

You're smart and you want to be smarter, you're good and you want to be better, but you don't really understand why the kind of advice I give to elite traders or hedge fund managers can possibly have meaning for you. What does their business have to do with yours? Don't they operate in an entirely different ballpark? And aren't these the same guys who blew up and lost billions of dollars in the most recent stock market meltdown?

The answers to those questions are both yes and no. Yes, top traders are probably handling much larger sums of money than you on a daily basis, and yes, many of them did lose a lot of money when the market went into free fall. But no, not all of them blew up, and not all of them are crooks. Some of them (those who happen to be my clients) are coming straight through the eye of the storm with the same high level of integrity they have always had, and while their ship may be beaten up a little, it is still very much intact and sailing strong.

More important, however, this book isn't about how to invest and make millions in the stock market. I leave that to the countless others who choose to write about some system or strategy they've found for making money in the markets. This book is about how super-successful people *think*. Because how they think is the key to how well they do. And the big news is that you can learn to think that way, too.

True success begins with a state of mind. But it takes specific actions and behaviors to move from intentions into action and get results. The eight principles outlined in this book are those used by all top performers in every field of endeavor—be it sports, business, politics, education, or anything else they choose to pursue.

I know this because my own career took several twists and turns before I found myself working with mega-traders as a peak performance coach. I started out as a clerk on the floor of the Chicago Mercantile Exchange and then eventually became a trader on the floor of the Chicago Board of Trade. When I left trading after three years because a herniated disc in my lower back made it incredibly painful for me to stand all day on the trading floor, I was sort of at loose ends—as we all are from time to time. My contemporaries were graduating from law schools, medical schools, or MBA programs and already building their careers, and I felt like the loser who had just wasted three years of my life. My work experience as a floor trader is not really a transferable skill in the real-world job market. I had no idea what I was going to do next, but I thought about being a baseball coach because I'd played Division 1 baseball when I was a student at Colgate University. The only problem with that career path was that I found out I'd need a master's degree if I wanted to coach on the college level. I wasn't thrilled with the idea of having to go back to school, but when I found out about the field of sport psychology I was intrigued enough to pursue it. My rationale was that since the commissioner of baseball at the time was a lawyer by training, I could certainly be a baseball coach with a degree in sport psychology. I knew it would be a long time before I made much money, but if I'd learned one lesson on the trading floor, it was that money can come and go very quickly, and, in the end, if you don't love what you do you won't be successful over time.

While I was still in graduate school I was offered an internship with the University of Connecticut baseball team. It was while I was working with the members of that team as a sport psychology consultant that the lightbulb went on. I realized that everything I was doing to coach a slumping batter out of his funk I could have used to coach myself when I was trading and bummed out because I was losing money. The psychology was exactly the same. Once I figured that out, I knew I was onto something: the difference between being a winner and being a loser has at least as much (if not more) to do with mental attitude as it does with your particular skills.

That's when I put together the proposal for my first book, *The Trading Athlete,* and started to make a name for myself as the first person with trading experience and a degree in sport psychology to apply that knowledge to improving performance in the trading world.

Since then, in addition to coaching my clients one-on-one, I've conducted hundreds of workshops for thousands of people working in financial institutions, multibillion-dollar hedge funds, and corporations across the country. I do a weekly video blog for CNBC and have appeared on the *Today* show, CNBC's *Fast Money*, *Squawk on the Street*, *The Call*, *Power Lunch*, *Street Signs*, *Closing Bell*, *On the Money*, *The Big Idea with Donny Deutsch*, *Millionaire Inside*, and many other programs, as well as on VH1's *The Fabulous Life*. And in each of my workshops as well as on television I've discussed the principles I'll now be teaching you.

The point is that I didn't teach baseball players how to hit the ball, and I don't teach my clients how to invest. Those are skills they already have. What I coach them on is how to think so that they can do what they already do well even better. And with this book, I can do the same for you.

This doesn't mean that if you're tone deaf I can teach you to sing opera; I can't. I am not a magician. I don't create talent; I simply help people to achieve their own potential. But if you have a great operatic voice and you want to take your career to the next level, the skills I teach in this book will help you to do that—so long as you're willing to commit to the program and walk the walk. The people I work with are already extremely good at what they do. But they aren't happy with just being A- players. They want to get an A+ and they'll commit to doing whatever it takes to get to that level. In that respect they're like bodybuilders who, to the layman's eye, look as if they have a perfect physique but who see room for improvement in themselves, even if it is just losing that last one-quarter percent of body fat. And because they see the opportunity, they are compelled to make the mental, physical, and personal sacrifices required to achieve that level of excellence.

For my clients, being good enough just isn't good enough; they want to be the best. It's not my job to advise them on seeking more balance in their lives or help them deal with their personal relationship issues. That's the work of a life coach or even a therapist. I am not a life coach, I am not a therapist, and I am not a licensed psychologist. I am a peak performance coach who is hired to help the elite identify areas for improvement, map out a plan of action, and then hold them accountable so they can achieve it.

The interesting thing is that, in most respects, these high fliers aren't any different from the rest of us. They're all flawed human beings, just like you and me—in some cases even more so. The one thing that does set them apart is that they've learned to *think* differently from most people. You can learn to think the way they do; it isn't magic—you've just got to want it badly enough to stop making decisions that are based on pure emotion or instinct and start to stick to your game plan, even when it's the last thing you want to do. (In fact, that's when you need to stick to it the most.) Then you need to get comfortable with the idea that you will be uncomfortable at times and will be taking risks—although, if you follow the rules I'm going to lay out for you and stick with the plan, they will always be smart, calculated risks.

I'm not saying that every decision you make is going to turn out exactly as you'd planned; that simply isn't realistic, and even the most successful traders know they're not going to make money on every trade. I'm not saying that you'll never make a mistake; what I am saying is that you won't be making any more stupid, avoidable mistakes.

The people I work with on a daily basis are the Tiger Woodses, Roger Federers, and Jackie Joyner-Kersees of the trading world. Confidentiality prevents me from disclosing their names or identifying their companies, but I can assure you that they are the ones who have been around for years and not only survived but even thrived during the global financial meltdown of 2008 and 2009. They are the stars that shine brightest in the trading universe, and I'm going to let you in on how they think. Make no mistake: It isn't their superior mathematical skills or their extraordinary good luck that's gotten them where they are. It's their thinking that makes them remarkable and solidifies their place in the supertraders' hall of fame.

So, welcome to the inner circle. The door is unlocked. All you have to do is gather the courage and determination to walk through it and use what you are about to learn.

Note to Readers

In order to avoid the awkwardness of having to write "he or she" or, even more awkward, "s/he" throughout the book, I've taken the liberty of using the male pronoun throughout the book. I ask all female readers to forgive me.

Principle #1

Find Your "Why?"

—————

A person who has a why can deal with any how.
—Friedrich Nietzsche

Darren is one of my first and most successful clients. I met him years ago when I was doing a workshop at a hedge fund. At the end of the session Darren approached me and introduced himself.

"I liked your presentation," he said. "I want to be great."

Now, this was a pretty sloppy-looking guy. His shirttail was untucked, he needed a haircut, and it didn't look as if he'd shaved that morning. But I knew better than to equate grooming elegance with success, especially in the trading world, so I asked him the same two questions I ask all my clients: "Why have you chosen to trade for a living?" and "Why do you want to be great?"

"What are you talking about? Why wouldn't I want to be great?" he shot back, looking somewhat annoyed.

"Well," I persisted. "You already make a ton of money, so why do you want to get to the next level? What's the point?" I was baiting him, but he had a ready response.

"Because I can. Because it's there to be achieved."

I knew Darren believed that, but I wanted to know more; I wanted him to dig deeper. We all know that greatness is there to be achieved, but not all of us are motivated or willing to take the risks to achieve it. So I kept on questioning.

As we continued to talk, it became clear that he thrived on the excitement, the fact that there were always new challenges, and the satisfaction of playing the game and solving the puzzle. He told me that when he was growing up, no one had expected him to amount to very much and he wanted to prove to himself that they were wrong. He understood that the business he was in was a meritocracy in which the upside was unlimited and no one else could determine his worth or limit his success.

By the end of our conversation I knew Darren was well on his way to greatness. He'd already taken the first step by identifying his "why," or what I call his core motivation. It was not a question of whether he had good reasons or bad reasons. All that mattered was that he had reasons for doing what he was choosing to do for a living.

Most people would assume that for high-flying traders like Darren, the motivation is all about money, but that is flat-out untrue. In fact, I've never had a trader tell me he was doing it only for the money. Most of my clients are so rich that if it were only about the money they could easily have retired years ago and still have amassed generation-changing wealth to pass on to their children. But, in fact, they're still trading. So it's not for the money. They do it for the excitement, the challenge, for the satisfaction of figuring the odds and making decisions with imperfect information. They love the game. They like to win. If they could make even more money in some other job than they do trading and were given the choice, they'd pick trading every time.

You'll be hearing more about Darren as you read on, and you'll also be meeting other mega-traders who've found their way to great by using these eight principles to unlock their potential.

I'm assuming that because you're reading this book, you, too, want to do better at "something" and you're curious to know how these mega-successful traders do it. You might even doubt that what works for them will work for you, but it will. In truth, it doesn't really matter what your "something" is because the first step is always to ask yourself *why you're doing what you do*. If you don't understand your core motivation, you won't know what's driving your engine, which means that you won't know what buttons to push to rev up the power you need to get to the next level.

Stop Asking Yourself "How?"

The reason most people go through life with big dreams but fail to achieve them is because they ask themselves "how" before they know their "why."

How am I going to grow this business?
How am I going to get that promotion?
How can I become a more effective salesperson?
How can I increase my income?

Those questions aren't very different from asking yourself:

How am I going to lose twenty pounds?

How am I going to find the time to go to the gym?

How am I going to get everything done that I need to do today, tomorrow, this week, this month?

What happens when you ask yourself those "how" questions? Do you feel more energized and determined, or do you begin to worry and fear that you can't or won't be successful? I'm betting it's the latter, because "how" is a question that's bound to bring up negative feelings. Instead of getting you excited, it leaves you deflated, with the result that you may decide not even to try. If I've just described the way you think, don't worry, because Principle #6 is going to teach you how to get past your fears and emotions so that you can put your "why" to work and improve your performance. But first you need to figure out what your "why" really is.

What's Your Why?

Maybe you can come up with an answer to the question of why you do what you do right off the bat:

I'm a marketing executive because I really get a kick out of figuring out what will influence people to buy one particular product rather than a competing one.

I'm a financial adviser because I like helping people plan ways to create financial security for their families' future.

I'm an entrepreneur because I love the process of taking a concept
from my head and turning it into a money-generating business.

I'm a news reporter because I really enjoy being on the front line of
global events and I get a real charge out of people's depending
on me for information.

I work at a coffee shop because I like to meet new people all day
long and really enjoy seeing the smiles on my customers' faces
when they smell and taste that fresh, hot cup of joe I brewed
especially for them.

I'm a teacher because it's so gratifying to see the light in my students' eyes when they learn something new and I know that I've
just created lasting growth in a young person's life.

As for me, I'm a peak performance coach because I love helping
people to unlock their abilities so that they can achieve greatness in
their performance.

If you are able to identify your "why" immediately, that's great.
You're reading this book because you want to do what you love more
effectively. But not everyone can answer so definitively or so quickly.
Maybe you really don't know why you're walking this particular
path. Maybe you've never really thought about it before—I know that
Darren, the client I told you about earlier, never had until I asked
him. Or maybe you knew once upon a time when you started out,
but now it's hard to remember because somewhere along the way you
got distracted and lost focus. In today's world that's very easy to do.

At the height of the economic meltdown of 2008, Darren (under-
standably) was not very happy, and asking questions like "How did
this happen?" and "How are we going to turn things around in the

next few months?" I reminded him that when we first started working together, I had asked him what motivated him as a trader. By this time, Darren's business had grown exponentially. He employed more than seventy-five people, and instead of the $30 million he was trading when I first met him, his fund now managed several billions of dollars.

"You asked me that?" He seemed surprised.

"Yup," I replied. "Five years ago I asked you why you wanted to get to the next level."

"And what did I say?"

"You said you wanted to be the best you could be because you loved the challenge and excitement, you loved playing the game and solving the puzzle."

"I did?"

"Yes," I repeated. "And in the midst of everything that's been going on around you—the market volatility, the fact that you're losing money right now—you temporarily lost your focus and have been asking "how" questions. You forgot why you were doing this in the first place. The challenge is still there, and more than ever there are puzzles to be solved. You just need to get back in touch with your 'why.'"

Even the most motivated and successful trader can get so caught up in the daily drama that he forgets this core concept. If you're having a hard time remembering why you got where you are in the first place, you need to take a step back and remind yourself of why you're doing whatever it is that you do. I tell my clients to write down this simple question—*"Why am I doing this for a living?"*—and then go home and think about it. I've never met one who couldn't come up with an answer. Sometimes their initial response is to say they do it for the money, but because I know that really isn't the whole story, I tell them they haven't really thought hard enough. They need to dig deeper. When they do that, they come up with the real answers: They do it for the excitement, for the challenge, because they like to win. They do it because no one else determines how much they're worth or puts limits on how much they can make. They are the masters of their own destiny. That is the real reason behind their true "why."

Try it yourself. Write down these two questions:

- Why have I chosen to (do whatever it is that you do)?
- Why am I still doing it?

Don't answer right away. Really think about it. Remember, your "why" is ultimately what's going to get you from where you are now to where you want to be.

It's quite possible that this simple exercise is all you need to re-capture your old passion. But there is still another possibility. It could be that you're doing what you do simply because you fell into it or because you inherited a family business and took the path of least resistance. Maybe you really hate what you're doing but just don't know how to start doing something else.

Does your answer sound like one of these?

- I am a teacher because my mother always said it was a good career and I get the summers to myself.
- I am a marketing executive because the money is good; I've been in marketing since my first job out of college; this is the only thing I know how to do.
- I'm a government employee because I know I have job security.

- I'm a department store manager because I spent a long time working myself up from salesclerk and I don't want to lose that seniority.

If so, can you see the difference between these "whys" and the examples on pages 10 and 11 that really communicated drive and passion. These responses are all about obligation, routine, and fear. Once you understand that all-important difference, you'll also understand why one kind of "why" is more likely than the other to lead to satisfaction and success.

If your responses to "why" are driven by a sense of obligation, complacency, or fear, you still need to find the "why" that will ignite your passion and set you on a different path. Ask yourself questions like "What do I really want to do with the rest of my life?" and "Is there something I've always wished I could do but was afraid to try?" Whether you've literally lost your job and are, therefore, being forced to reinvent yourself, or whether you've simply lost your way, you now have a great opportunity to harness your core motivation and move in a new direction.

Asking these questions will help you figure out your "why," which will, in turn, drive you to determine "how" and then do whatever it takes. It doesn't matter whether you're twenty-four years old and just starting out or whether you've been pursuing a career for half your life. If you want to do better, you can. If you want to do something different, you can do that, too. And the sooner you figure out your "why," the sooner you can start to do it.

> *Why* will motivate you to succeed.
>
> *Why* will keep you going when you encounter setbacks.

Why will push you to continue when others are telling you to quit.

Why will keep you energized when your body is begging you to stop.

Why *Why* Works

There's nothing magical about why *why* works. It's all a matter of perspective. Knowing why you want to do something shifts your perspective from the negative to the positive. Instead of getting that sinking feeling in your stomach because you're asking, "How am I ever going to be able to do this?" you'll be buoyed up by knowing, "I *have* to do this because . . ." Knowing your "why" is what's going to get you to figure out how.

Knowing "why" takes you from wanting or wishing to willing, from desire to execution. You may wish you'd gotten your MBA or want to go back to school to get it, but knowing *why* you want that degree is what's going to get you off the sofa and into night school. Perhaps you've always wished you could open your own business instead of working for somebody else, but it's knowing *why* that will give you the courage to quit your job and tend bar a couple of nights a week if necessary until the money starts coming in. No matter how much you may want or wish for something, you've still got to pick up the oar and start rowing the boat to make it happen.

Passion Is the Path to Peak Performance

Achieving excellence isn't about finding more balance in your life. Remember, I'm not a life coach. Nor am I a spiritual guide. I'm a peak performance coach. And the way to achieve peak performance is to devote yourself totally and completely to doing whatever it is you feel most passionate about—no matter what hurdles you have to jump, what setbacks occur, or what doubts you may have from time to time about your ability to achieve it.

There's a wonderful anecdote that illustrates this point very well. As the story goes, a woman went up to the world-renowned violinist Isaac Stern after a concert and gushed, "Oh, Mr. Stern, I'd give my life to be able to play the way you do!" To which Stern replied gravely: "Madam, I have."

I said at the beginning of this book that my peak performance trading clients don't trade only for the money. It's important for you to keep that in mind because this fact lies at the heart of why you need to discover your "why."

There's a reason you've chosen to do whatever it is you do to earn money. But is money the only reason that you are doing what you do? If so, discovering your "why" will enable you to think differently about what you're doing. What if you're a lawyer but you've always wanted to be a fitness instructor? Fitness instructors don't make as much money per hour as lawyers, right? But what if you used your legal skills to establish your fitness training business and put all your passion and drive into creating the next super-successful national chain of fitness centers? If you did that you'd be following your passion *and* making a lot more money than you probably would as a lawyer.

I'm not telling you that every decision you make is going to turn out the way you'd planned. Even the most successful traders make a profit on their trades only about 53 percent of the time. What I am telling you is that learning to think like these super-successful traders, embracing and implementing the principles they follow day in and day out, will put you on the path to becoming better *and* more successful at whatever it is you're most passionate about.

So before you turn the page to the next page, get out an index card or a notebook or your BlackBerry or computer and write down these two questions:

- Why have I chosen to do what I do?
- Why am I still doing it?

If you don't know why you're still doing what you're doing, you probably need to ask yourself a third question:

What would I rather be doing?

Give these questions some thought—you may not come up with definitive answers right now. After all, you are only at the beginning of this process. (In fact, learning to love the process is one of the key principles in this book. But more on that later . . .) Meanwhile, keep these questions—and the answers you've come up with—in mind as you read on.

PRINCIPLE #2
GET TO KNOW YOURSELF

I think self-awareness is probably the most important
thing toward becoming a champion.

—BILLIE JEAN KING

I f you've already discovered your "why," you've actually taken the first step toward knowing yourself better.

Really getting to know yourself is the foundation of everything else you're going to be learning and doing from now on. And I'm not talking here about rediscovering your inner child or getting in touch with your feelings. I'm talking about the kind of self-awareness that allows you to acknowledge both your strengths and your weaknesses so that you can use them to balance each other and keep yourself from going overboard in either direction. Self-awareness allows you to do more of what you're good at and less of what you're not. It can also send up the red flag that lets you know you're about to do something stupid.

The perfect trader—if such a person exists—is methodical and careful about making decisions, extremely disciplined, resilient to setbacks, with a high degree of internal confidence. He holds strong opinions but is also able to admit quickly when he is wrong, not take it personally, and view it as a learning opportunity rather than a failure. He understands the value of leaving his ego at the door. He's willing and able to trust his gut and place big bets when the opportunity presents itself. In fact, that pretty well describes the ideal blend of characteristics of any successful person, no matter what he is doing professionally or personally.

But I've met very few traders—even among the most successful—who are hardwired with all these skills. What they do all have, however, is a high degree of self-awareness, which allows them to make the most of their strengths and minimize the impact of their weaknesses—which, by the way, is why I know that with the right coaching any good trader can become great, and any great trader can become elite. In fact, every one of the qualities I mentioned above results from mastering a teachable skill that can be acquired and applied by anyone to virtually any endeavor.

Let's go back to our good friend Darren for a moment. Darren is a brilliant trader, but there are only so many trades any one guy can handle by himself. And since he wanted to become great, he knew that the only way to grow his business was by taking in more traders. But Darren is a terrible manager of people, and he knows that. He could, of course, have spent a lot of time trying to become a better manager. But that would have meant taking away time from doing what he does best—analyzing the market and making smart trading decisions. In any case, Darren didn't really want to be a manager. So he made a wise decision: he brought in a COO to recruit new traders and run the daily operations. That gave him the opportunity to play to his strength while neutralizing his weakness (interpersonal relationships), which is the formula that allowed him to increase his business from $30 million to several billion dollars in just a few years.

You Don't Have to Change Who You Are

I would never ask Darren to change who he is, even if he were capable of doing that, any more than I'm going to be asking you to try to become someone you're not. First of all, it probably wouldn't work, and second, it isn't necessary. What I am going to do is ask you to take the time to sit down in a quiet place with a pencil and paper (or at your computer) and make a list of three to five strengths and three to five weaknesses you think you have as a person.

A lot of people have trouble with this because they haven't spent a lot of time practicing introspection, so here's a short list to help you get started. Just remember that these are not all the strengths and weaknesses in the world, and you will probably come up with many that I haven't noted here.

Strengths

Decisive	Analytical	Supportive
Focused	Optimistic	Calm
Curious	Persuasive	Organized
Smart		

Weaknesses

Easily distracted	Intolerant	Too softhearted
Introverted	Procrastinator	Lazy
Afraid to take risks	Indecisive	Forgetful
Poor sense of time		

People are generally pretty good at beating themselves up and putting themselves down, so you'll probably find it a lot easier to own up to your weaknesses than to describe your strengths. Don't be afraid to give yourself points for what you're good at.

If you find you need help or validation, ask your spouse, partner, or a friend who knows you well and whom you trust to tell you about your strengths. *Just don't ask anyone with whom you are really close to name your weaknesses.* As I've said, you can probably come up with plenty of those on your own, and asking someone else to point out your faults will probably only lead to hurt feelings or an argument.

Once you've made your two lists, it's time to move on to the next step—and this is where it really gets interesting and enlightening.

Get a New Perspective

First, take your list of strengths and, for each one, ask yourself these two questions:

- How can I use this particular strength to help me to do better?
- How can this strength get in the way of my doing better?

Let's say, for example, that one of your strengths is the ability to remain calm in the midst of crisis. Obviously this will help you to stop, step back, and make good decisions when those all around you are losing their heads or becoming paralyzed by fear. But how can it hurt you? Well, it may be that because you're so calm you don't always convey the true urgency of a situation when you need someone else to take action. Then, when you follow up and discover that it wasn't done, you may be told, "Oh, but it didn't sound like you thought it needed to be done immediately. You didn't make it seem that urgent."

Here's another: Maybe you've pinpointed being organized as one of your core strengths. Being organized is essential, especially in today's complex business environment. It helps you to set priorities, to keep track of many things at once and move logically from one project to the next. But people who are very organized also run the risk of spending so much time making sure they've got all their ducks in a row that they never get to the point of putting their plans into action. So once again, one of your core strengths is both an asset and a liability.

Here's a sample of how one of your entries might look:

Strength	How It Helps	How It Hurts
1. Calm	Able to keep my head in crises	Don't convey urgency to others
2. Organized	Helps me to set priorities	Spend too much time on putting things in order

Once you've analyzed each of your strengths, it's time to examine your weaknesses in the same way. For each weakness that you've identified, ask yourself:

- How can this weakness get in the way of my doing better?
- How can this weakness help me to do better?

In this case you may have identified forgetfulness as one of your weaknesses. It's pretty obvious that not remembering what you're supposed to be doing or whether or not you've already done it can put a major crimp in your ability to function at your best. But knowing that you have a bad memory can force you to make sure you write things down and review your "to do" list on a regular basis, which can really help to keep you on track. And you'll have pretty comprehensive notes on your activities, which can be very beneficial.

Or maybe you tend to be intolerant. That tendency can mean that you don't delegate responsibility and prefer to do it all yourself, but it might also mean that you demand the best of the people with whom you work, which will keep them working at optimal levels at all times.

Once you're finished, you should have a chart that looks something like this:

Weakness	How It Hurts	How It Helps
1. Forgetful	Can forget deadlines	Makes me double-check
2. Intolerant	Don't like to delegate	Demand the best of others

Here's how Sean, one of my clients, assessed his strengths and weaknesses:

Strength	How It Helps	How It Hurts
1. Excellent memory	Quickly recognize patterns in the market	May lose objectivity and think I see patterns that are not really relevant
2. Highly analytical	Able to objectively analyze data and not get distracted by size of trades or money involved	May fail to listen to what my gut is telling me and occasionally miss great market opportunities

Weakness	How It Hurts	How It Helps
1. Hardworking	Potential to experience burnout	Willing to put in long hours and push myself to severe limits
2. Hate to keep track of details	Can fail to follow up when I should	Do not get lost in minutiae and can concentrate on the big picture

Now it's your turn. Get out your notebook or turn on your computer and make your own list of strengths and weaknesses. Then write down how each of them can either help or hurt you.

Make your lists as exhaustive as you can—and then go back and add some more. The more qualities you are able to articulate, the better you'll come to know yourself, and the better able you'll be to use your self-knowledge to your advantage.

If you can't think of a reason why a strength might also be a weakness, you're probably letting your ego get in the way of your objectivity. (You'll be learning more about how to avoid that particular pitfall in Principle #6, Keep Your Cool.) And if you are having trouble thinking of a reason why a weakness might also be a strength, consider how you compensate for that weakness (like the person who takes notes because he feels he is forgetful) and then find the strength in that action.

Self-awareness Creates Checks and Balances

I suspect that even if you've been aware of the assets and liabilities you bring to the table, you've never been asked to look at them in quite this way before. It's an exercise I go through with every one of my clients for two important reasons.

First, this exercise allows you to see something that is very familiar to you from a different perspective. My trading clients do this all the time; it's a critical part of the process they use in order to make great trading decisions. For this example, I will use stocks in the stock market. Before a top trader decides whether or not to buy a stock, at a certain price, he asks himself why someone else would want to sell it at that same price. (Remember that this business is called trading because for a trade to occur every buyer must be matched with someone who is selling at the same price, and vice versa.) If a trader is making a new investment, assumably he's buying because he thinks the stock will increase in value while the seller is willing to sell the stock at that same price because he thinks it will decrease in value. If the potential buyer can't think of any good reason for the other guy's belief that the stock will decrease in value, he'll have even more reason to consider the stock a good buy. The buyer already has his own opinion because he's done his research.

But looking at the other side of the coin and seeing how something good might be bad is a way to make sure his decision remains objective and is not based on ego or emotion.

To put this concept in another context, imagine that you are the CEO of a major corporation. If you surround yourself only with people who you know will agree with whatever you say, you'll be denying yourself the opportunity to see things from a different perspective. If, on the other hand, you listen to people who tell you what they really think, you'll be creating a system of checks and balances. In the end you may still decide to do it your way, but at least you'll have considered other possibilities.

The second reason is that determining where your strengths and weaknesses lie, and looking at them from a new perspective, is a way to create checks and balances for yourself so that you don't go careening too far off in one direction or another when you're moving forward.

Once you become aware of your tendencies you'll be able to recognize a warning sign when you see it and put on the brakes before you crash or do something stupid. Being emotional, for instance, can really keep you energized and fully invested in what you're doing, but making impetuous decisions based on emotion is a liability in almost every situation. If you know that you tend to get caught up in your emotions and you feel yourself beginning to get carried away—say, you are in the midst of a negotiation and you hear yourself getting agitated and talking louder and faster—you can stop yourself, take a deep breath, and even walk away for a minute or until you calm yourself down.

If you've ever watched a Grand Slam tennis match you've probably seen a player get really upset when he misses a point or thinks a call has gone against him. He might even throw down his racquet (or use it to smack himself on the head), but then he needs to let it go, calm down, and not let his emotions get in the way of the next point. Great players know how important this is, and they know how to get themselves back to being focused. It's just one of many characteristics elite athletes share with elite traders. And again, it isn't magic; it's just a kind of discipline anyone can acquire in order to join the ranks of the elite.

Do You Need Help with This?

Some people have a harder time than others defining their strengths and weaknesses. If you're finding this exercise more challenging than you think it should be, there are two tests you can take to help you out: the Myers-Briggs Type Indicator and the Keirsey Temperament Sorter. You can take the Keirsey test free online at www.Keirsey.com, but there is a fee for taking the Myers-Briggs, which has to be given by a qualified administrator. I'm not saying that you need to take one of these tests, but you certainly can if you think it would be helpful. Whatever you can do to know yourself better will work to your benefit as you pursue your goals.

Self-knowledge Is a Powerful Thing

Alexander Pope famously said, "A little learning is a dangerous thing." To turn that maxim around and put it in the context of our current discussion, the more you are able to learn about yourself, the better able you'll be to put that knowledge to work for you in all your endeavors.

You'll be using your self-knowledge to determine what sets you apart from others in your field (Principle #4), to determine your own value without comparing yourself to others (Principle #5), and to stop yourself from allowing your ego and/or emotions to get in the way of your objectivity.

Keep reading to find out just how often you'll be revisiting what you've learned about yourself to create and maintain that all-important edge in any competitive market.

Principle #3
Learn to Love
the Process

One may walk over the highest mountain
one step at a time.

—Barbara Walters

All winners know that there are two kinds of goals—long-term outcome goals and short-term process goals—and that to achieve our long-term goals we need to focus on the process.

Sometimes when I give a seminar or workshop, I like to start off with an interactive activity. I call for a volunteer to come up to the front of the room and hand him a fistful of colored pens. I explain that those pens represent all the things he has to deal with on any given day. The blue one is the report that his boss has been breathing down his neck to get finished. The red one is the birthday present he still hasn't bought for his spouse. The green one is the rotisserie chicken he promised to pick up for dinner on the way home. The orange one stands for the prescription for new glasses he needs to get filled. And so on. Then I ask him to throw all those pens up in the air and try to catch them on the way down. Sometimes he can catch a couple at random, but most of them just wind up rolling around on the floor. That little demo usually gets a good laugh, but it also makes a serious point.

We all have a multitude of tasks, obligations, and requests coming at us every day, and if we don't set our priorities and complete one thing at a time, we'll be doing the equivalent of trying to catch a whole bunch of pens at once, which simply isn't possible. What we need to do instead is lay all those pens out in front of us and pick up one at a time, do what we need to do with it, and then set it aside. In other words, we need to create a plan that allows us first to establish priorities and then to focus on one thing at a time. We select a task, get it completed, and then move on to the next one. We'll still have as many tasks to handle but by focusing on one at a time and filtering out all the distractions we'll be engaging in *process thinking,* which is the only way to achieve a desired outcome—in this case, dealing with all those obligations and completing every task.

I said at the beginning, when I asked you to find your "why," that I was assuming, since you were reading this book, you had some kind of long-term goal, something you wanted to do differently or better. Maybe by now you've refined that, or even changed it, based on what you've already learned—it really doesn't matter because, whatever your long-term goal may be, the key to achieving it will be to set short-term goals and focus on the process of completing one at a time.

What Is Your Vision?

Where do you envision yourself being a year from now? In five years? Ten years? It's a question most people hate being asked because it forces them to speculate about the unknown. Nevertheless, you need to have a vision for yourself before you can determine how you're going to achieve it. For someone like me it's seeing this book piled on a front table at my local bookstore or getting on the *New York Times* best-seller list and then having that success lead to a number of regular, high-profile media appearances that will eventually develop into *The Dr. Doug Show* on daytime television. In my mind, all of this has already happened; time has just not caught up with it yet.

For a trader the vision might be multiplying his yearly profits by a particular percentage. A golfer might envision himself winning a major tournament. A vision gives you something to work toward, but it can also be a bit scary. People are afraid to think big because they're afraid it's not going to happen. *Oh, no, not me! That could never happen to someone like me!* My answer to that is, *Why not you?* Of course it can happen to you. The people who achieve great things are human beings just like you and me. If one person can do it, any other person can do it, too.

Don't believe me? Then consider the story of Miami native Devon Rifkin, 2008 winner of *Entrepreneur* magazine's Entrepreneur of the Year award. By his own admission, Rifkin was "a terrible student." After squeaking through high school he attended Tallahassee Community College for six months before dropping out.

After a short stint as a stockbroker in New York City, Devon went to work for his father, whose business was supplying stores with fixtures and display materials such as mannequins, racks, and lighting. One day a local shop owner came into Devon's father's store and purchased five hundred dollars' worth of hangers. "Wow," thought Devon, "that's a lot of money to spend on hangers." He saw a need, did his homework, refined his idea, and in 2000 launched the Great American Hanger Company, which in 2008 did more than $10 million in sales.

So, yes, if it could happen for Devon, it can also happen for you. That said, however, the tricky thing about visions is that they're not entirely under your control. I can't control how many people buy my book. The trader can't control the market or the economy. The golfer might get hurt and be unable to play. But that vision should always serve as the incentive to keep going even if you have to modify the specific steps (the process) needed to improve your odds of achieving the ultimate goal.

Devon didn't just have a vision—I don't think there's anyone who has a vision of starting a hanger company. Unconsciously, he applied all eight of the principles outlined in this book. He found his passion in entrepreneurship (Principle #1). He knew his weaknesses—academics—and his strengths—salesmanship (Principle #2). He set goals and took the steps necessary to establish his business (Principle #3). He used his edge (Principle #4) by applying the knowledge he'd gained working for his father and doing his homework. He had internally based confidence (Principle #5). In a recent interview with the *Miami Herald* he said, "A lot of people could be successful if they weren't afraid of failing." He has kept his cool (Principle #6), following the process to get where he is, and he is comfortable with the fact that there is always risk involved in making decisions (Principle #7). *Entrepreneur* magazine quotes him as saying, "I started with nothing. So to go out there and really let it rip and to grow this great thing without being hesitant and having that confidence—I think that sets us apart." Finally, it seems that after a shaky start in college, Devon is now holding himself accountable for his decisions (Principle #8).

To get to the next level and to achieve your long-term goal you can't just snap your fingers or click the heels of your ruby slippers together like Dorothy in *The Wizard of Oz* and wish it were so. You need to put yourself on the line, commit wholeheartedly to the process, and do whatever you can to *make* it happen. It takes discipline, commitment, determination, a willingness to take risks—and, most important of all, a structure and a plan.

Define Your Goals

I tell my clients that once they've articulated their vision, they need to define their short-term goals—the little steps they're going to take to get themselves where they want to be. And I make them write down these steps. I know that writing stuff down can be a bore, and you've got about a million things you'd rather be doing, but getting to the next level isn't about doing what you want to do; it's about doing what you *need* to do. And actually writing down your goals not only helps to clarify them, it will also serve to intensify your commitment to the process.

As you've already seen, I love to flip things around to help people get a new perspective. Why? Because once you begin to think about things differently, you're more likely to do things differently. If you don't shift the way you think, you probably won't change the way you act. Or, as Henry Ford put it, "Whether you think you can or you think you can't, either way you're right."

The more you think like a winner, the more likely it is that you'll act like one, too. If you think you'll never achieve your vision, you are probably right. You won't. What are your goals? When you got up this morning was your goal to oversleep, to skip a workout, to miss breakfast, be late to work, be totally miserable all day at your job, eat an unhealthy, fattening lunch, leave work as soon as possible, and come home to slump down in front of the television, feel sorry for yourself, eat a quart of ice cream right from the carton, and watch some mindless reality television show? Was that your process? If so you've probably achieved all your goals for the day, and they certainly got you closer to your vision, which was, after all, to not achieve your vision. Congratulations.

So I ask you again, what are your short-term goals? What is the step-by-step process you're going to use to achieve your vision? If you're still at a loss, here's an acronym I use to help clients structure and define their goals: **C.H.A.M.P.®**. Goals must always be **C**ontrollable, **H**ard, **A**ccountable, **M**easurable, and **P**ositive.

Controllable means that the ability to achieve a short-term goal is completely within your control. So, for example, if I were a professional baseball player, my goal shouldn't be to hit .300 for the season because there are too many other people and factors involved in determining my ability to achieve that (coaches, umpires, pitchers, injuries, weather, and so on). Instead, my goal should be to train hard all season, stay focused when I am hitting, and swing only at good pitches, because I have complete control over all of those variables.

Hard means that your goals should be slightly out of reach so that you have to keep pushing yourself to reach the next, higher level of performance. If goals are too easy to achieve, we tend to become bored or complacent, like the kid in your class at school who always seemed to get A's without trying but who tended to get into trouble because he was bored and needed to make things more interesting for himself.

Accountable means that if you don't have the discipline to make yourself do what you've committed to, you need to find someone else to whom you will answer. (We'll be talking more about how to do this in Principle #8, Make Yourself Accountable.) The point is simply to achieve your goal, so whether you hold yourself accountable or call on someone else to hold your feet to the fire doesn't really matter. Most of us do things that are difficult or even unpleasant because we know there will be a consequence if we don't. Pushing yourself isn't always easy, or what you necessarily want to do. But it's what you *need* to do to achieve your vision, so asking to be held accountable by turning to someone else isn't a sign of weakness; it's an indication that you know yourself.

Measurable means that you need some objective way to track your progress. The surest way I know to do this is to keep a daily or weekly performance journal that not only shows you in black and white what progress you've made but also lets you know how and when to modify your goal if necessary as you work toward achieving it. (I'll be talking more about the journal in Principle #8.)

Positive means that you always state your goals in positive terms by telling yourself what "to do" rather than what "not to do." So, instead of saying, "My goal is to not be late to work anymore," you should say, "My goal is to get to the office early so that I get a jump start on the day." Laugh if you want, but as a peak performance coach, I have yet to see anyone achieve his goals by thinking in negative terms. Negative thoughts create negative behaviors; positive thoughts generate the potential for positive outcomes.

Commit to the Process

One of the most compelling illustrations of how setting short-term goals and committing to the process leads to extraordinary achievement is the story of how Roger Bannister became the first person ever to run a mile in under four minutes. At the time, many people believed that running a sub-four-minute mile was humanly impossible, but Bannister had a plan. He ran with two pacemakers. The first pacemaker, Chris Brasher, ran under the four-minute pace with Bannister slotted in behind him for the first half mile. Then, when Brasher began to tire, Bannister signaled to his second pace-maker, Chris Chataway, to take over. Chataway moved up and ran under the pace with Bannister right behind him until they were two hundred yards from the finish, at which point Bannister sprinted ahead and crossed the finish line in 3 minutes, 59.4 seconds.

The point is, Bannister didn't start out saying he had to run the mile in under four minutes. Instead, he had short-term goals—keeping up first with Brasher and then with Chataway—and when those two things were added together, Roger found himself being the first person to break the "impossible" four-minute mile. Even more interesting is the fact that once Bannister had done it, everyone realized it was possible to achieve, and within months more and more people began to break the four-minute mile. Even a high school junior from Wichita,

Kansas, did it in 1964, and in 2001 a senior from Reston, Virginia, became the first high school student to do it indoors.

> *Whether you think you can or you think you can't,*
> *either way you're right.*
> —HENRY FORD

Don't Get Distracted

If you allow yourself to get distracted, you're likely to abandon the process and start making stupid, self-destructive decisions—like trying to catch all those colored pens at once. We'll be talking more about how to stay cool in the midst of chaos when we get to Principle #6, but for now I just want to emphasize how important it is to concentrate on the step you need to take right now and not trip yourself up by looking too far ahead. In sports, that's keeping your eye on the ball at all times. For traders, it's thinking one trade at a time.

There's hardly anyone these days who doesn't have some kind of budget to meet. It might be bringing in a certain number of dollars or selling X number of units or signing Y number of new clients by the end of the fiscal year. In effect, those are all visions because no one can really control how much money they bring in or how many units people will buy or how many new clients will want to sign with their company. The only thing you can do is create a step-by-step process that is *within your control* for achieving your vision. And once the plan is in place you need to trust it and stick with it. If you don't, as the fiscal year is drawing to a close and you still haven't reached your budgetary goal you may start to make *un*smart, emotional, off-the-cuff decisions hoping that enough of them will turn out to be good so that you'll make your budget after all. In the end, that is irresponsible behavior and generally leads to failure.

The best traders don't think about how many millions they need to make that year. They focus on making the best trading decision they can with each trade they make. And if there isn't a good trading opportunity right now, they have the discipline to do nothing and just wait. Concentrating on one trade at a time is their process.

Compare this way of thinking to the way Tiger Woods thinks when he's on the course. He doesn't think about how many—or, actually, how few—strokes he needs to win the tournament; he thinks about making the best shot he can every time he addresses the ball. As Dr. Patrick Cohn, president of Peak Performance Sports, said in an interview with the *New York Daily News,* Tiger is "able to fully immerse himself in the execution of each and every shot without attaching consequences to it, thereby letting the results come to him." Similarly, when they're standing at the plate, the greatest hitters in baseball don't think about how many home runs they need to break the record; they think about waiting for the pitch that's right for them and swinging at it rather than just swinging at whatever comes along.

Sticking with the plan and going with the process takes discipline, but ask any one of the most successful traders on the street and he'll tell you he'd much rather lose money on a trade he'd made for the right reasons than lose money on one he'd rushed into or had doubts about when he made it. You see, while losing money is not fun, top traders understand that it is a natural and even necessary part of the game that they play. As a result, top traders don't actually mind losing money; what they really mind is losing money doing stupid things. Similarly, ask any elite athlete and he'll tell you that while losing is not fun, he understands that losing (just like winning) is a normal part of competition and therefore he would much prefer to play great and lose rather than make stupid mistakes and lose.

Recently I saw a segment of a program called *How It's Made* on the Discovery Channel that was about how toothpicks are mass-produced. It's a process that's repeated over and over again, starting with a tree and winding up with the same number of the same size toothpicks in identical little boxes. At first the technology is sort of interesting, but after a while it's just boring to watch. To an outsider, "playing" the financial markets probably sounds sexy and exciting, but in reality, if you are a talented and profitable trader, it isn't so different from mass-producing toothpicks. The best traders make one trade after another, following the same process each time, over and over, day after day, month after month, year after year—and doing that can actually become pretty tedious. Therefore, they have to avoid letting boredom lure them into trying to make things more exciting for themselves, because that's when they are likely to deviate from the process and start getting into trouble by doing stupid things.

Another challenge is to stick with the process and stay on track even when they're up big money and ahead of the game, so to speak. Not so long ago, one of my clients who trades in commodities was up 15 percent on his portfolio halfway through the year. Most traders get paid a fixed percentage of what they make in trading profits for the firm and they only get paid once, at the end of the fiscal year. They don't receive a regular paycheck like a normal job. It really is an "eat what you kill" occupation. In fact, a trader can be up millions of dollars in December and if he loses it all before the year ends, he will likely get paid nothing for his efforts of an entire year of work and still have to make back any losses he incurred before he can get paid in the next year. So, as you can see, being up lots of money by midyear can frequently cause a trader to want to stop trading for the remainder of the year so he can protect his profits and get paid out on them. Because my client was up 15 percent already, he was on track to receive a very large paycheck at year end and his instinct—because he is, after all, human—was to go on vacation for the rest of the year so that he wouldn't give in to the temptation to make more trades and so run the risk of giving back (that is, losing) what he'd already made. That's when he called me, because he knew himself well enough to understand that he was getting scared, and he couldn't allow himself to make a fear-based decision.

Traders aren't paid for making a particular number of trades; in fact, they shouldn't *ever* trade just for the sake of making a trade. So they could theoretically "take a vacation" whenever they hit some earnings goal they'd preset for themselves. But, as I reminded my client, top traders also commit to a process. In this case, I suggested that it might be a good idea, based on his situation, to raise his economic vision for the year. After all, how could he have predicted at the beginning of the year how highly the market would reward his strategy, and who could say that there was not more money to be made? The point was that taking a six-month sabbatical just because he was up big money sooner than he expected was not the right thing to do.

Traders, like athletes, who take time off run the risk of losing their rhythm and timing. But also, like a batter standing at the plate with a 3 and 0 count, a really great trader who is way up on his earnings for the year knows he should become even more selective in terms of the risks he's willing to take. The batter with a 3–0 count would and should swing only at what he considers to be the perfect pitch. If he does that, even if he hits the ball hard and gets out, he's able to jog back to the dugout with his head up, saying, "That was my perfect pitch. I get paid to swing at those pitches, so I had to swing at it, and unfortunately I cannot control what happens after I hit it." Similarly, the elite trader who has surpassed his profit expectations for the week or month or year should only make a trade when the risk/reward ratio is so distinctly in his favor that it would be irresponsible for him *not* to make the trade.

What this means is that you, too, may need to adjust your goals and expectations from time to time and fine-tune your process, either because you're doing better than expected or because what you're doing isn't working as well as you'd planned. (I'll be talking about exactly how to do that in Principle #5, Be All That *You* Can Be.)

The process is what keeps you from acting out of fear—whether it's because you're worried that you won't meet a goal or because you don't want to lose the advantage you've gained. It's what keeps you thinking like a smart trader rather than becoming a gambler just because you want to keep things interesting and what prevents you from doing nothing because you're afraid of doing something wrong.

So what you need to do is stop right here, define your short-term goals, and commit to the process.

Now, go back and review the C.H.A.M.P.® rules I laid out earlier in this chapter. Do each of your goals meet those five criteria? In your notebook or on your computer, create a chart for yourself like the one below and write them down. And then, using a simple "to do" list, map out the process you are going to follow in order to achieve those goals. Keep this chart someplace where you can refer to it on those occasions when you're tempted to break your own rules and stray from your commitment to improve.

My Goal	Is It a C.H.A.M.P.® Goal?	Yes/No
	Is it *Controllable?*	
	Is it *Hard?*	
	Am I *Accountable?*	
	Is it *Measurable?*	
	Is it *Positive?*	

My game plan for achieving these goals is as follows:

Do What?	When?
Review my sales for the past six months to determine which of my products are selling best	At the end of the first six months of my fiscal year
Revise my manufacturing plan for the next season to determine what changes need to be made	Within one week of the completion of my six-month sales review

. . .

By now you've found your "why," determined the strengths and weaknesses that will help you figure out "how" to realize your vision, and committed to the process of setting and achieving your short-term goals. But there's still one more aspect of self-discovery for you to explore. That is finding and using the edge that's going to tip the odds in your favor and guarantee success in whatever it is you want to do. In the next chapter you'll learn why the motto "No edge, no trade" can and should be applied to every decision you make from now on.

PRINCIPLE #4
SHARPEN YOUR EDGE

If you don't have a competitive advantage,
don't compete.

—JACK WELCH, FORMER CHAIRMAN OF GENERAL ELECTRIC

Your competitive advantage is whatever tips the odds of success in your favor, whether you're competing against another person, determining how to make the correct decision, or planning a strategy. When the combination of odds and potential payoff is in your favor, you have the competitive advantage.

I grew up in Miami, Florida, so I spent a lot of time saltwater fishing in the Atlantic Ocean. Now, I realize that most people wouldn't think of fishing as a competitive sport (although there are actually fishing competitions), but it occurred to me that trying to catch fish is an appropriate analogy to explain what it means to have an edge. So please bear with me for a moment while I tell my fish story.

One day I decided to go fishing with a friend who was visiting from Colorado. He'd done a lot of lake fishing, but he'd never fished in the ocean before. We were standing next to each other on a boat anchored about a mile offshore. There was a lot about the situation neither one of us could control—the strength of the current that day, the weather, how hungry the fish were. But because I'd fished in these waters before, I knew that ocean fish generally bite for shrimp. So I'd brought along a bucketful of live shrimp, and once I cast my line, I sat back and waited. My friend, however, had decided to bait his line with worms because the freshwater fish in his lake back home bit for worms. Unfortunately for him, he hadn't done his homework, so he didn't know that worms don't work in the ocean— just as I am pretty sure my shrimp would not work in his lake. (And since I'm a competitive kind of guy, I wasn't about to tell him.) After a couple of hours, my bucket was full of fish and my friend, who'd caught nothing, was frustrated and annoyed.

The only reason I caught fish and he didn't was that I knew more about ocean fishing, and that information created my competitive edge. Had he done his homework or had I revealed what I knew to him at the beginning of our fishing expedition, I would no longer have had the edge that allowed me to outfish him that day.

Two Sharp Edges Are Better Than One

Gaining a competitive advantage is like having a two-edged sword, and you need to keep both of them sharp. One edge is internal— knowing what unique skills you bring to the table. The other is external and comes from gathering knowledge that makes it more likely you'll succeed. The most successful people, like successful fishermen, keep both edges finely sharpened.

What Is Your Inside (Internal) Edge?

At this point I'm going to ask you to refer to the lists of strengths and weaknesses you made during Principle #2 because you need to figure out how to leverage "who you are" to improve your odds of reaching your goal.

Maybe, like Sean, whose strength and weakness assessment appears in that chapter, you have an excellent memory (which for Sean means he can quickly recognize and recall patterns in the market) but you hate all the detail work. If you know that, you can hire people who are detail-oriented to do what you're not good at so that you're free to do what you do well. By doing more of what you're good at and finding a way to neutralize what you're not so good at, you'll be increasing your edge in the marketplace.

An edge can comprise several components that come together to set you apart. Take me, for example. There are other peak performance coaches working in the financial sector, but none of them has the same exact combination of skills that I do: background as an athlete and a floor trader, education (Ph.D. in psychology specializing in sport psychology), experience of working with high-end traders and hedge fund managers, and strong communication skills. When I entered this business, no one who had graduate-level training in sport psychology was applying that knowledge and theory to the trading world, even though everyone in the business was using sports analogies to describe what they did. (Interestingly, the firm I'd traded with in Chicago recruited almost exclusively from the Illinois and Wisconsin University athletic programs.) So my particular combination of experience and expertise constitutes my competitive edge.

When you know yourself, you can use that knowledge to create an edge. If you're good with people, for example, you might decide to give out your cell phone number and tell clients to call you directly with any questions or problems. Giving them that kind of access would be a definite competitive advantage, particularly in this world of e-mails and texting.

The key is not to change who you are but to enhance and encourage whatever you can use to set you apart from the pack.

Your Personal Edge Is a Sales Tool

Basically, at the end of the day we're all selling something, whether it's ourselves, our product, or our service. But before we can make a sale, we've got to market our product and develop a customer base. Your internal edge is the bait that's going to lure the fish onto your line as opposed to the line of the guy sitting next to you on the boat.

In an interview published in *Forbes* magazine in 2007, Donald Trump was asked to name the greatest book he'd ever read. "*The Art of the Deal* by Donald J. Trump," he replied, apparently in all seriousness. "It was a great read in 1987, a number one best seller then, and nothing has changed."

Trump is actually one of the greatest marketing geniuses around. His internal edge is not his outstanding knowledge of the real estate market or the fact that he's a Wharton graduate; it's the outstanding size of his ego, which he's used to leverage himself and his company to the status of an internationally recognized brand and then shamelessly promote it. Trump's greatest sales tool is Trump. Whether it's a hotel, a residence, a casino, a golf course, a clothing line, a reality TV show, or Trump vodka (and, by his own admission, he does not even drink alcohol), what he's actually selling is himself—a

Brooklyn-born, street-smart, swaggering tycoon with really weird hair—which has become, oddly enough, part of his iconic image. Donald Trump truly believes he's larger than life and has managed to convince millions of others of this fact.

Not everyone has the personality or the desire to become The Donald, but everyone has something he can use to make him or his product unique. If you're a pediatrician, what's going to make me take my children to you instead of the other pediatrician in town? Assuming you're both good doctors, it might be that you have more toys in your waiting room or a Nintendo Wii game system or more convenient office hours. If you're a public speaker, what's going to draw in the crowds? Is it your message or your humor or your entertaining delivery? If there are two gourmet coffee shops equidistant from your home, what makes you decide to buy coffee from one rather than the other? Assuming they both use the same coffee beans, what will make you decide to frequent one more than the other? Maybe it's that one has Wi-Fi and the other doesn't, or maybe one has friendlier baristas.

In a world full of choices, establishing an edge can make the difference between success and failure in whatever you do.

Delivering on Your Promise— Sharpening the Outside (External) Edge

The second component—or edge—of your competitive advantage lies in making sure that you gather as much information as you can and use it to make the best decisions in order to maximize your opportunities to deliver the best product or service. I call this your external edge because the information is "out there" to be had, but you need to go after it. For a trader that means having a repeatable process he follows each time he makes an investment decision. The most successful traders always make decisions based on the most accurate if necessarily imperfect information they can gather, and they make a trade only when that information lets them know that the risk/reward ratio is in their favor. Their mantra, which is translatable to all decision making, is "No edge, no trade."

When You're Taking a Risk, Think Like the Casino

Taking a "smart" risk means gathering as much information as you can to be sure that you are more likely than not to profit from a decision. This is the opposite of gambling. If you're wondering what the difference is, let me explain.

When you go to a casino, every single game is statistically designed so that the odds for success favor the casino—and are therefore against the person playing the game (aka the gambler). This means that the casino always has the mathematical edge. In fact, the most successful traders I know never go to casinos because they are aware that the odds are against them. As one of my clients named Scott put it, "Why would I play a game that, over the course of time, I have no chance of winning? Yeah, I might get lucky, but when it comes to making decisions about money, I don't rely on luck."

Before I started to work with elite traders, I'd always assumed that trading was a lot like gambling since they both seem to involve fast action, quick money, and having a stomach for risk taking. In actuality, however, the two could not be more different. As my client, Scott, correctly pointed out, gamblers may get "lucky," go on a perceived "hot streak," or "have a system" to make some quick money, but, in the end, they will never have the true mathematical advantage, and so, over time, they will lose. Remember, it is not a question of "if" they will lose more than they make. It's a mathematical fact that eventually they *will lose*. Maybe not today. Maybe not tomorrow. But it will happen eventually because the numbers don't lie and the casino has the edge, not the gambler.

Let me assure you that there is a good reason casinos give high rollers free rooms and free meals, and it's not because the casinos think those high rollers are nice people (although they might be). It's because the casinos need to keep the gamblers gambling so the "house" (aka casino) can continue to make money. Even if the casino makes only pennies on the dollar, all those pennies add up over time. And they will add up, because the casino has the edge.

Casinos are masters at exercising their edge. Even in a game like roulette, where the odds *appear* to be even, the casino still has an edge. How? Well, on a roulette wheel, half the numbers are red and half are black, half are even while half are odd, half are high and half are low. So it would appear that if you make one of those so-called "even money" bets, your odds of getting it right are fifty-fifty. But an American roulette wheel also has one green 0 and one green 00 (European wheels have only one 0, so the house has slightly less advantage), and when the ball lands on one of those, *all* the even-money bets lose. Those green spaces where you could place your chips on the table are very cleverly positioned to look different, and they are relatively hard to reach, so the average player naively thinks that the ball is somehow less likely to land on one of them. In actuality, of course, it's statistically just as likely to land in one of those slots as it is to land on any one of the other thirty-six slots on the wheel.

And those green spaces mean that rather than having an eighteen in thirty-six—or 50 percent—chance of winning, you actually have only an eighteen in thirty-eight—or 47.4 percent—chance, while the casino has a 52.6 percent chance. That's a 5.2 percent difference in the casino's favor. This gives them a clear edge over you, which means that the casino is always going to be the winner on even-money bets over time. Great traders think like the casino, not the gambler.

What does this mean in the real trading world? If one of my clients has been hearing rumors that lead him to suspect something big is going to happen at some particular company and that would increase the company's market share and, therefore, its stock price, what would he do? He wouldn't buy the stock immediately because the rumor just "might" be true. He would first do his due diligence, gathering as much information as he could (short of engaging in insider trading) by speaking to as many people as possible in the industry who are familiar with the company as well as to the company's competitors to determine the likelihood that whatever he'd heard was really going to happen. That level of information gathering would give my client a leg up on other traders who are trying to find out the same thing. Then he would use what he'd learned to assess the risk involved in the potential trade. He'd run all the numbers, do all the calculations, and come up with what the financial world calls a "model."

Based on this careful analysis, my client might think there was a 70 percent chance this big event was going to happen, and if it did, he might speculate that the stock price of the company in question would go up by two dollars. But that would also mean there was a 30 percent chance it wasn't going to happen, in which case, again based on his calculations, the stock price would go down one dollar. According to that model, if my client were to buy a million shares, he would have a 70 percent chance of making $3 million and a 30 percent chance of losing $1 million. Given those parameters, the client would know he had the edge and would be compelled to make the trade. After all, who wouldn't want to place a bet or play a game when he had a 70 percent chance of making three dollars and only a 30 percent chance of losing one dollar for every dollar you risked? Of course, he still might lose money, but the best traders know that if their edge is good and if they play only when they have the edge, in the long run, over time, they will make a profit, just like the casino.

Taking Smart Risks

Most people are terrified of losing money or of making a bad decision because they don't know how to figure out when they have an edge, which means that they don't know when they're taking a smart risk. Elite traders, on the other hand, are not afraid of losing money, because they know that's going to happen about half of the time. But they also know that if they play only when they have the edge, they'll be making good decisions and their gains will, in the long run, outweigh their losses.

To show you what I mean, I'd like to play a little gambling game with you. No need to take a trip to Vegas; all you need to play this game is a quarter. Now, flip the quarter. You call it, and if you get it right, I will give you twenty dollars. But if you get it wrong, you have to give me twenty dollars.

Would you want to play that game?

In a game like the one I suggested, you'll never have the edge. Every time you flip the quarter the odds will be fifty-fifty. You might either make or lose money on the first flip or even the first few flips, but if you kept flipping from now until the end of time, in the end, mathematically, you'd always eventually break even. So what's the point of playing?

Oh, I can hear you already. Your mind is spinning scenarios where this is a good gamble: "But I just might get lucky. . . ." Now you're thinking like a gambler. Sure, you might get lucky from time to time, just like the proverbial blind squirrel who just might find nuts once in a while, but that poor little squirrel will probably starve come wintertime because, unfortunately, he has to rely on luck, and luck is not edge. Top traders play the game when they have the edge and only when they have the edge because their goal is to consistently put themselves in a situation where they will have the greatest possibility for success. If that means they have to be patient and wait, then so be it, because they know that the way to succeed is by having a competitive advantage and playing it big when that advantage appears. In any business model, if you just keep guessing or hoping that you're going to get lucky with every decision you make, over the long haul you're going to be wrong as many times as you're right, which is not what anyone would call a good business model or a recipe for success.

Now let's take the coin game one step further. Would you change your mind about playing the game if the rules were that if you win, you get one dollar, and if you lose, you lose one dollar? How about if you win, you get ten thousand dollars, and if you lose, you lose ten thousand dollars?

If you think you would play when all you could lose was a dollar but not when you stood to lose ten thousand dollars, you are about to make a bad decision because you are now personalizing what *you* view as a large or small amount of money and that is influencing your decision to play the game or not. My clients do not think that way and that is what contributes to their ability to be successful.

It doesn't matter how much money is at risk in this game, because the fundamentals don't change. It is still a 50 percent chance to win and 50 percent chance to lose the game and the payouts are still equal so you don't have any edge. No edge, no play. Top traders view risk as risk, and it doesn't matter if there's $1, $1,000, $1 million, or $100 million at stake. It is still about probabilities and payouts. The rest is just a bunch of zeros.

Even when there's $10 million riding on a trade and everyone's natural instinct is to be uncomfortable, if the *combination* of probability (that is, the odds) and payoff (that is, how much you make when you are right as opposed to how much you lose when you are wrong) is in their favor, traders force themselves to go for it. Notice that I didn't say simply when the *odds* are in their favor; if the odds seem good but the potential loss is disproportionate to the investment, the risk still wouldn't be smart. Traders know that they need to calculate both the odds *and* the potential payoff based on the best, most complete information available in order to have the edge. In the end, it's all about being objective, doing the math, and following what the numbers tell them. The process they go through *every single time* before deciding whether or not to make a trade is this:

Probability x Potential Payout = Expected Return

Now, let's go back to that example of the trader who had a 70 percent chance to make $3 million and a 30 percent chance to lose $1 million, but instead of talking in terms of millions, let's use three dollars and one dollar. (Remember that for traders the numbers, no matter how big, are just part of the game.) As we discussed, this was a great bet. After all, the odds *and* the payout were in his favor. Unfortunately, bets like that don't come along too often. Instead, we are usually faced with situations that are not so clear-cut. So now let's suppose that instead of having a 70 percent chance to make three dollars, this trader had a 70 percent chance to make only one dollar. And instead of a 30 percent chance to lose one dollar, he had a 30 percent chance to lose three dollars. Should he make that bet? And what if we changed the scenario yet again so that he had a 30 percent chance to make three dollars and a 70 percent chance to lose only one dollar. Does that feel like a good bet? Before you look at the chart below, write down whether or not you think each of these scenarios is a good bet so you can see if the math agrees with you.

Scenarios	Good Bet or Bad Bet?
70% chance to make $3 and a 30% chance to lose $1	
70% chance to make $1 and a 30% chance to lose $3	
30% chance to make $3 and a 70% chance to lose $1	

Now let's look at what the math tells us.

Probabilities (odds)	(X)	Payout	=	Expected Return	Net Expected Return	It is smart to make the bet?
70% 30%	(X) (X)	+$3 −$1	= =	+2.10 −.30	+1.80	YES!
70% 30%	(X)	+$1 −$3	= =	+.70 −.90	−.20	No. Even though you have a 70% chance to win, it is not a good bet.
30% 70%	(X) (X)	+3 −1	= =	+.90 −.70	+.20	Yes. Even though you only have a 30% chance to win, the math tells you it is still a good bet.

As the chart shows, math does not lie. It isn't affected or changed by what a person thinks, feels, or wants. And for that very reason he knows that sticking with this process is what's going to wind up getting him to his ultimate goal.

You won't necessarily be doing this detailed level of math each time you make a decision, but we all do some form of analysis quickly in our heads when we decide whether to do something or not. But to make sure that you are making the best decision possible, you will need to look at the odds and the potential payoff in an objective manner to be sure that your choice is not emotionally based. In fact, you don't have to be a math expert to understand this principle. Here's another example of how to assess smart risk that comes from the world of baseball.

I don't know what you think of Barry Bonds's home run record, and for our purposes it doesn't really matter because I'm more concerned with the number of walks he earned than with the number of home runs he hit. Although it's not what made the headlines, Bonds actually holds the Major League record for career walks—a total of 2,558, which is 537 more than Ted Williams and 469 more than Babe Ruth. Bonds achieved that record by demonstrating extraordinary discipline when he was at bat and swinging at a pitch only when he knew it was at just the right place in the strike zone to put the odds of success in his favor. If he didn't get the pitch he was waiting for, he didn't swing, which is why he had so many walks. Every time he was thrown a pitch, he instantly calculated his chances of hitting the ball solidly. That was his process of gathering the best information he could in order to determine whether or not he had the edge. In Bonds's case, that was a pretty quick calculation (he only had about .2 seconds), but it involved the same kind of objective information a trader is acquiring when he has to make a trading decision or that you need when you make any kind of business decision.

Four Questions to Determine Your Overall Edge

Remember that your overall edge is determined by leveraging your strengths, minimizing your weaknesses, and then gathering as much information as you can before making a decision. Translated into terms that are applicable to whatever your own situation might be, you need to ask yourself the following questions in order to determine your edge:

1. Given my strengths and weaknesses, my experience, the business environment (and whatever else you can think of to factor into the equation), what are the odds that I'll succeed in whatever it is that I'm contemplating?
2. What is the realistic upside if I do succeed?
3. What is the realistic downside if I fail?
4. Is the net payoff (upside minus downside) positive or negative?

That's your process. Once you've answered those questions, you'll have calculated whether or not you're taking a smart risk. If you do that every single time you make a decision, it will work for you the same way it works for top traders, top athletes, and top businessmen.

Principle #5

Be All That

You Can Be

———

I do the best I know how, the very best I can;
and I mean to keep on doing it to the end.

—Abraham Lincoln

You probably recognize this chapter title from television commercials as the United States Army's onetime recruiting slogan. I think it delivers a powerful message by urging people to look inside themselves and become peak performers by literally being all they can be.

Most people don't do that. Instead, they spend a lot of time comparing themselves to, and worrying about whether they're doing better than, their neighbors. *Is my house nicer than theirs? Do I have the right cars? Are my kid's clothes as trendy as what the other kids in his class are wearing?* Why is it that so many people spend so much of their emotional capital worrying about these things? In truth, top performers—on and off the Street—don't waste time doing that.

They have a more compelling way of measuring success, which is to compare themselves to their own *absolute* standard of excellence.

You might think that if Stan the Salesman in the next cubicle made one hundred thousand dollars in sales last quarter and you made one hundred fifty thousand dollars, you were doing really well. But Tom the Top Trader doesn't judge his own performance according to what Nick the Trader Next Door made last month; all he thinks about is what he could or should have made, given the market circumstances. So, if in a given year the market presented him with opportunities he could have optimized to make, say, $75 million and he made only $10 million, by absolute standards he didn't do as well as he could have—no matter how well or poorly Nick the Trader Next Door might have done.

If you're judging your own success in terms of someone else's, you may be doing comparatively well but possibly not the best you can. You could very well be settling for less than you're capable of accomplishing. In fact, it's essential for top traders to keep challenging themselves, because, judging in comparative terms, they're already doing so well that they'd have no reason to keep trading each day. Instead, they look at what level of opportunity the market presented on a given day, or in a given week, month, or year, and determine whether they'd taken full advantage of those opportunities. Did they hesitate to make a trade they should have made? Did they rush to buy too soon? Did they fall victim to their emotions and get out of trades too soon rather than learning to tolerate the pains of their gains and hold the position longer? If so, they weren't working up to their potential. These guys judge their performance not only in terms of how much money they made but also in terms of how disciplined, controlled, or aggressive they were in making their trades. In other words, they calibrate their "success" in terms of their own potential.

We've already discussed the fact that even when a trader has met or exceeded his self-imposed financial goal for the year, he must continue to follow the process and continue to trade. If he were to take the easy way out and went on "vacation" instead of staying in the game, he wouldn't be doing as well as he could—even if, in the end, he wound up losing some of that profit. That may sound illogical, but you need to remember that for these guys, when they have the edge they *must* make the trade, even though they are very much aware that it's always possible to lose money on a good trade. And the same criteria should apply to you if your goal is to do the best you can by taking advantage of every opportunity, regardless of what the next guy is doing.

If You've Already Got Enough, Why Try for More?

If you think you're "good enough" or that you're doing "well enough" at whatever it is you've chosen to do with your life, maybe you don't need to be reading this book. If you don't want to get better, nothing here can motivate you to improve. That has to come from within. But I can tell you that top traders never feel that way. Words like "mediocre" or "average" are like daggers to their soul. They don't want to be "good enough," and they're constantly challenging themselves because they will never be satisfied to remain at their present level. They will do just about anything and make whatever sacrifices are necessary to get better because being anything less than the best they can possibly be is unacceptable. And again, I have to emphasize that what's motivating them is not the idea of making more money— or at least not in the same terms you and I think about money. For them money is just a vehicle they need in order to continue doing business in much the same way a basketball player needs a ball to shoot hoops or a shopkeeper needs inventory to sell.

At the time of the writing of this book, one of my clients is down 4 percent on his profits for the year. In the current global financial crisis, if he were to compare himself to what others are doing, he'd have to believe he was a rock star because his peers are down 20 to 30 percent. Some are down even more than that and either have had to shut down their businesses or are at risk for having to shut them down. Even at a time when the major stock indexes are off almost 40 percent from their yearly highs, my client doesn't measure his own performance in those terms; he's not going to think it's okay to be down just because everyone else is. That would be thinking comparatively, and he, like all top performers, holds himself only to his own absolute standard of excellence. So, rather than patting himself on the back for doing better than Nick the Trader Next Door, my client is going to think about what opportunities the market is offering so he can take smart risks and not only make up the 4 percent he's down but also get ahead of the game. He's going to keep on trying to be the best *he* can be, regardless of what the competition is doing or not doing.

Running a Personal Best

Do you know how that feels? No? Well, imagine that you run in a race and wind up coming in first, but when you look at the clock, you realize that you've run your personal slowest time ever. Would you be happy that you'd won the race or disappointed that you ran your slowest time? If you answered that you'd be happy, you are focused on relative comparisons. If, on the other hand, you answered that you'd be disappointed, you are among the few who are focused on absolute returns and being the best you can be, regardless of the outcome.

But why does it matter that you didn't run as fast as you could, since you did, after all, win the race? The answer to that question takes us back to the issue of goal setting. You need to be in control of achieving your goal, and you can only control how *you* prepare for and run the race. In this case you happened to win, but that was just luck because you didn't run your best and you cannot control how the other runners do. Thinking only in terms of what *you* are capable of doing is thinking absolutely, and that is how my top trading clients think about and judge their performance.

No one embodies this kind of internal motivation better than Tiger Woods. As of this writing Tiger has won an astonishing eighty-nine tournaments, sixty-five of them on the PGA Tour. At the ripe old age of thirty-three, his lifetime earnings top $82 million (not to mention his endorsements and product sales, which put his earnings in the hundreds of millions). What is it that keeps him going, and winning, even when he has a torn ACL and two stress fractures in his left leg, as he did when he won the 2008 U.S. Open? It must be the money, right? Wrong! The secret he shares with other top performers is that he never goes out on the course to beat someone else. Odd as this may sound for someone who has spent the last several years beating other elite athletes, the one Tiger consistently tries to beat is himself. "He's competing against himself. He wants to be perfect," said Yankees captain Derek Jeter in an interview with the *New York Daily News*. "When you see tournaments, he'll be up twenty strokes and he wants to win by thirty. It's not just a matter of, 'Hey, lemme go out here, I've already won, let's finish it up and move on.' He wants perfection. That's why he's been so good."

The same can be said of Annika Sörenstam, who holds the record for the most Player of the Year awards on the LPGA Tour and who many are calling one of the best female golfers ever. When asked by *NCGA Golf* magazine about her preparation for playing with the men on the LPGA Tour at Colonial in 2003, she said, "I had set goals and had a plan with each practice. During the week I could focus on just being Annika. When I joined the Tour and won my first tournament I was being compared to Nancy Lopez. It's tough to fill Nancy's shoes and that was never my goal."

The difference between challenging yourself to be the best you can be and just trying to beat the next guy is that excellence is a constantly moving target, so you'll always have something to work for. You won't be tempted to rest on your laurels and you won't be distracted by looking all around you when you need to be focused on your own performance. Another golf great, Ben Crenshaw, once said, "You have to play your own game . . . That was the hardest thing we had to do playing against Jack Nicklaus. You end up watching him and it affects your concentration."

That's not to say, however, that my clients aren't aware of how others are doing or that I'm telling you to pluck the estimation of your own value out of thin air. I used to write a regular column for *Trader Monthly*, a trade magazine that has now ceased publication. Many top hedge fund managers have told me they never read it because they felt it focused on the glitz and glamour rather than the nuts and bolts of the business. Interestingly enough, however, the one issue they always read was the *Trader Monthly 100,* which listed the top hundred earners of the past year in the hedge fund industry. I know this because I saw it on their desks or they made reference to it during our conversations. The question is, then, if they are so focused on their own performance and claim not to care how others are doing, why did they read it? They read it because, unlike baseball or any other sport where averages are tracked and published on a regular basis, *Trader Monthly 100* provided the best information they could get about how they were doing relative to their peers. It was a way to let them know whether they needed to step up their own game. They used it as a frame of reference, to make sure they were in the right ballpark in terms of their own performance. That doesn't mean, however, that if they were making more than another guy running a similar fund they would relax and bask in the glory of beating a competitor. What it does often mean is that if they found they weren't doing as well as their peers, they might take that as a cue to reexamine their own business model and investment process in order to sharpen their game. Remember, for these elite talents, complacency and mediocrity are both unacceptable choices.

Confidence Should Come from Within

Internally based confidence means that you always get into the game believing you're the best, regardless of how well anyone else is doing. It means that you determine your own value and don't settle for less. Whether the product you're offering is a car, an opinion, a talent, or a stock portfolio, being the best of the best means that you never rely on other products or other people to determine your own worth. You determine your own value and come to the table prepared to walk away if the client or customer isn't willing to pay the price.

This may sound like hubris or plain old arrogance, but it isn't. The truth is that some cars drive better than others or have higher-quality parts, some opinions are more valuable than others, some performers are more gifted, some singers are better, some traders are more profitable, which means, in every case, that they deserve to be valued and compensated more highly.

Going back to our golf analogy: Tiger Woods knows he's the best. Every time he enters a tournament he knows he's favored to win. So if another golfer beats him, that's a signal for him to go back and reexamine his own game. It doesn't mean he's going to start copying another guy's swing or using someone else's club selection for his tee shot, but he might think about what he could do to improve his own swing or rethink his own club selection because he knows he's capable of doing better than he did.

The Tiger Woods of the investment world is probably Warren Buffett. If I'm Warren and you're another investor, I know I'm savvier than you because I've proved it time and again over the course of many decades. Therefore, if this year you outperform me, I'll know I'm off my game because I've been outperforming you consistently over time. That doesn't mean I'm going to start copying your investment decisions. What it means is that I'll have to go back, reexamine my own investments, and decide for myself what I might be doing wrong or not seeing in the markets, and what I can do better in the future.

The elite in any field are independent thinkers. They don't care what *you* might think is right for them. They don't even care what you think is right for *you*.

I can hear what you're thinking: "Well, if I were Tiger Woods or Warren Buffett, I wouldn't worry about what anyone else thought, either." But here's the point: Tiger wasn't always Tiger Woods, and Warren wasn't always Warren Buffett.

The first four years Tiger played (1992–1995), his highest finish was at 41 and he didn't win any money. When he turned pro in August 1996 there were many golf experts who thought he was a young prodigy destined to crash and burn. But Tiger knew how good he was, he continued to play his own game, and now the world knows it, too. Why? Because his actions, consistent performance, and results have spoken for themselves.

When Warren Buffett took over control of Berkshire Hathaway in the 1960s it was a textile manufacturing company bucking increased foreign competition. Seeing the handwriting on the wall, Buffett looked to shift the company's focus by negotiating the purchase of two Nebraska insurance companies. By 1985 Berkshire Hathaway was out of the textile business completely and Buffett was using the insurance company's assets to invest in stocks and bonds. He didn't become the richest man in the world (according to *Forbes* magazine) by taking his cues from other investors. He did it by doing his homework (or due diligence), gathering as much information as he could about the companies whose stock he was considering. Of course, he watched and listened to what others were doing. But he did it to learn from their mistakes (and sometimes their successes), and in the end, he always made his own judgment calls and investment decisions. If the rest of the world thought he was crazy, so much the better, because Buffett could then do what he loves best—buying when everyone else in the world is scared and running for cover.

Don't Get Sucked into External Markers of Merit

Contrary to much popular belief, the most successful traders can be extremely insecure. It's often their insecurity that pushes them to ever-increasing levels of effort. Yet, ironically, the more successful they are, the more insecure they become. As the market keeps reminding them, "You're only as good as your last trade." And because of that basic fact, it's easy for even top traders to slip into accepting externally based validation from time to time. If the market pays them, they feel good about themselves. If the market takes money from them, it's easy for them to start feeling bad and to worry that they've lost their edge. And that's when I usually get a call.

There are a couple of exercises I go through with my clients that anyone can use to remind themselves how good they really are and recover that all-important, internally based confidence.

First, I tell them to write down the answer to the question "Why am I THE MAN?" and then read that answer to themselves every morning before they begin trading and again at the end of the day—as well as anytime they feel their confidence wavering.

Another self-affirming exercise we do is "Walk the Talk." For this one I have them walk normally across the room and take note of their body language. Then I ask them to think to themselves that they are *the* best, in full control, having a great day, on top of the world—and then show me that walk. Now when they walk they invariably exhibit a more confident posture and rhythm in their stride.

If you think this sounds silly or that you would feel foolish, just try it in the privacy of your own home. There is a clear connection between your mind and your body. If your mind tells you that you are weak, tired, lacking in confidence, your body will respond accordingly. If your mind thinks confidence, power, and self-esteem, that's what your body will show. And the connection works both ways, so if you're feeling anxious or doubting yourself, all you need to do is change your body posture—throw your shoulders back, lift your head up, and walk with confidence—to change your state of mind. If that sounds simple, it is, and, psychologically, it works.

On a purely rational level, my job as a coach is to remind my clients that they can't control the market and if they've consistently made smart, nonemotional decisions, whatever the results, they need to feel good about those decisions. If they've followed their own process and made a trade only when they had the edge (or, in Barry Bonds's terms, if they've swung only at *their* pitches), they did their job and, therefore, they need to feel good about themselves regardless of the outcome.

Here is another way to think about that. Suppose I told you I was playing in a baseball game and went 0 for 4, meaning I had four at bats and got out each time. Would you say that I had a "good game" or a "bad game"? Before you read any farther, circle one of these answers: Good Game or Bad Game.

Now, I am going to give you two scenarios to consider.

Scenario #1: I went 0 for 4 and struck out four times.

Scenario #2: I went 0 for 4, but in my first at bat I hit a line drive to third base and the guy playing third caught it. The second at bat, I hit a bomb and the center fielder caught it by climbing the wall like Spider-Man. The third at bat, I hit a dart up the middle and the shortstop laid out and gunned me down from his knees (yeah, I know I'm not a very fast runner). The fourth at bat, I hit a shot to left and the guy in the outfield chased it down and dove to make a great catch.

Now, let me ask you again: Did I have a good day or a bad day at the plate? Most people would initially think, "Well, if you went 0 for 4, you definitely had a bad day at the plate. After all, you never made it to first base." But then, when I reframe the question using those two scenarios, they would say, "In scenario one, you definitely had a bad day at the plate. But in second scenario, even though you got out four times, you hit the ball hard and had some great at bats."

My statistical average was the same in both scenarios: .000. However, let me ask you another question: Which scenario do you think would have given me more confidence going into my fifth at bat? Or tomorrow's game? Or, better yet, if you were the coach, which scenario would make you more confident about sending that player to the plate for his fifth at bat if the game were on the line? I think we would all agree that the answer is scenario #2.

This is an important distinction to make, because what my clients know is that all you can control is the pitches at which you swing (or trades you make) and that you cannot control how the players in the field play (whether those trades make or lose money). That is how they are able to keep internally confident no matter what their profits or losses are at the end of the day.

The takeaway lesson for everyone wanting to optimize their own performance without regard for what others are doing is fourfold:

1. Know your edge.
2. Act only when you have the edge.
3. Avoid taking the outcome personally because it involves factors that are beyond your control.
4. Measure your success in terms of how well you performed and not only the outcome.

Even when you're outperforming your peers and/or achieving substantial success, you need to continue following that formula. And if you're doing less well than the next guy, you still need to believe in your own abilities and not play Follow the Leader.

Having internal self-confidence will put you on the road to success, while seeking validation based on external circumstances is always the surest road to eventual self-destruction.

Principle #6
Keep Your Cool

In crisis management, you have to keep your cool;
otherwise people start thinking, "if he's scared,
maybe we better be."
—William McDonough, former president,
Federal Reserve Bank of New York

Keeping your cool means not letting your ego and emotions get in the way of making smart decisions. The higher the stakes, the harder it can be to do that, but top traders, regardless of whether they're making or losing big money, know they have to stay cool at all times if they want to keep their edge in the marketplace.

There's no question that the higher the stakes, the greater the anxiety you're likely to feel. If I toss a coin in the air and ask you to call it just for fun, you probably won't have any trouble picking heads or tails because the outcome doesn't really matter. Since there isn't any money involved, you don't have anything to lose—or gain. But what if I tossed that coin and bet you a thousand dollars on the outcome? You'd probably start to imagine what it would feel like to win or lose a thousand dollars in a few seconds. You might even start to fantasize about what you would do with the money if you won or what you would have to give up if you lost. The bottom line: you'll probably get a little anxious and have a harder time deciding how to make the call.

Of course, you already know from the previous chapters that no great mega-trader would take that bet, because the odds of winning a coin toss are never better than fifty-fifty and the payout on this game was equal (make a thousand or lose a thousand). But when you're making any kind of decision—or, more specifically, any *sound* decision—the most dangerous thing you can do is to allow yourself to become emotional or to get overly invested in the need to be right.

It's all about remaining objective, and you can use this principle as the basis for making every decision in your life, whether it has to do with your work life, buying a car, dealing with a personal relationship, or investing. Remaining objective may not guarantee that you win all the time, but it will absolutely guarantee that you don't lose just because you've done something stupid or emotionally driven.

But I know that you're asking, "Aren't there *some* decisions that *should* be based on emotion?" Let's look at something really personal, like who you decide to marry—assuming you want to get married. That is certainly one of the most emotionally driven decisions anyone could make. Interestingly enough, the statistics tell us that 50 percent of all marriages end in divorce, so at least half the time that emotionally driven decision appears to be a "bad" decision in the long run. Does this mean people should stop getting married? Of course not. But it might mean that if people engaged their heads in addition to their hearts and physical attractions when choosing a spouse, we might see more marriages that lasted a lifetime like the standard marriage vow of "until death do us part" suggest it should.

Sometimes Losing Is Winning

You can win when you're losing when you make the decision you *need* to make instead of the one you might *want* to make even though you know that decision might mean taking a painful loss. Since I'm writing this book in the middle of the monumental subprime mortgage crisis, let's look at an example related to the housing market. Suppose you'd bought a house a couple of years ago for $525,000. Now you're moving to a different state and you want to sell it, but the highest offer you've received is $350,000. (Bear in mind, I'm not talking about being forced to sell; I'm not talking about any doomsday scenario. I'm talking about making the equivalent of a sound business decision.) You let ego get in the way when you think the market is wrong and potential buyers are just trying to rip you off because there is *just no way* your house is worth that much less today. Or you might get emotional about the idea of losing 33 percent on your investment in such a short time (which would certainly make anyone a little sick to his stomach) and decide to turn down the offer, even though the market is telling you that this is now what your house is worth.

To avoid making that kind of emotional, ego-driven mistake, you need to step back and look at the situation objectively. It doesn't matter what the market was two or five or even twenty years ago; this is the market today, for better or worse. So you need to put yourself in the shoes of the potential buyer: If you didn't already own your home, what would *you* be willing to pay in today's market for a house like this? Once you are able to shift your perspective, it becomes crystal clear that there is no way you'd be willing to pay $525,000. So why would you expect someone else to want to pay that price?

If you really want to sell your house, $350,000 is what you're going to get. No one is trying to rip you off. The housing market isn't trying to cheat you. The market doesn't think you're smart or dumb. The truth is that the market has absolutely nothing to do with you personally. It reflects supply and demand and, equally important, the collective state of human emotions—greed, fear, or stubbornness. And you have very little control over the supply and demand.

Given those parameters, there are a number of questions you can ask yourself to determine whether or not you should take that $350,000 offer:

1. What are the odds that the price of the house will return to what I paid for it and how long could that take?

2. What are the odds of the price going up to more than I paid? How much more and how long could that take?

3. What are the odds of the price going down even more and how much lower could the price go?

4. If I carry the house long enough for the price to go back up to what I paid (or higher), how much will it cost me in cash each month and over the entire period of time?

5. Is there an opportunity for me to use that money to do something else that could be more lucrative?

6. Is there an emotional capital cost (losing sleep, feeling depressed, being angry) to my holding on to the house?

7. What makes me think I have a good reason to trust that my answers to all of the above questions are accurate? Is it how I feel, what I think, or am I just guessing? Am I an expert or, if not, have I done my homework by speaking to a number of experts in order to formulate a well-informed opinion?

If you answer those questions honestly and objectively, you'll be creating the kind of model top traders use whenever they consider buying or selling a stock or commodity.

Traders understand that the market doesn't know or care what they paid for a stock or commodity or how long they have held it. All that matters is what it's worth in the *current* market. So if they based their decisions on what they paid minutes, hours, days, weeks, or months ago, they'd be holding on to losers (like the homeowner who refuses to sell for less than he paid). But they know that the market is not out to get them—although it certainly feels like that. The market doesn't even know who they are or what investments they're holding. Top traders are able to maintain their cool and keep their egos, and anger, fear, greed, and other emotions in check because they don't take any of it personally. If they have to take a loss, they chalk it up to having bought at the wrong time (just as the homeowner bought at the wrong point in the housing cycle). To maintain their objectivity, they ask themselves these two questions:

1. If I didn't currently own this stock or commodity, would I want to buy it or sell it?
2. If I were to buy or sell it, what price would I be willing to do it at and why?

The same formula holds true for virtually any decision anyone has to make about when to cut their losses or even taking a profit. Whether you're selling a product or a service or making a lifestyle decision, the key is to stay cool, assess the situation like a scientist rather than an overemotional person, do what the data are telling you, and move on.

Knowing the Difference Between Need and Want

Deciding when to cut your losses is one of the toughest decisions for anyone to make, but traders at the top of their game know that they *always* have to make the decisions they *need* to make, which may or may not be the ones they *want* to make. They are *willing* to do what's necessary even when they don't want to. Does that homeowner want to sell his house for less than he paid? Does a trader want to take a loss on a trade? Of course not. But that's the way anyone who wants to excel in any kind of business needs to think. Doing what needs to be done, even if you don't want to, is just part of doing business. Nothing more, nothing less.

In the music world, artists very often don't want to perform the songs that audiences most want to hear. Bono, the lead singer from U2, has probably sung the song "Sunday Bloody Sunday" thousands of times over the years. After that many times, it is possible that he may never want to sing or even listen to "Sunday Bloody Sunday" ever again. But the reality is that this is the song that launched U2's career back in 1983 and made the band an international household name. Like it or not, the world has identified Bono and U2 with "Sunday Bloody Sunday," and every time he steps onstage, even twenty-five years, twenty-two Grammy Awards (the most of any rock band), and dozens of successful songs later, "Sunday Bloody Sunday" is the song Bono's fans want and even expect to hear at some point in the show. So Bono, the consummate professional, knows what he needs to do to keep the fans happy, and he includes this signature song in every one of his shows.

If gas prices are through the roof and you make automobiles, you may love SUVs but you'd better be making compacts and hybrids. If you manufacture women's clothing and purple is the big fall color, you might hate purple personally, but you'd be stupid not to include it in your line.

A top trader may "fall in love" with a stock and want to buy more even though (or maybe because) the price is going down. Or he may be tempted to take his profit on a stock that's on the rise because he wants to bank some cash. If he were to do either because it's what he *wants* to do, he'd be making an emotionally based decision. But top traders won't allow themselves to do that. They understand that they *need* to do whatever is in the best interest of their businesses. So, instead of increasing their position by buying more of a losing stock, they will show tremendous discipline and sell the loser, no matter how painful that might be. Conversely, if they're holding a position that's going up in value, they will endure the pains of their gains, battle their emotional desire for instant gratification, and hold on to the stock or even buy more because they know that the market is presenting them with the opportunity to take a really smart risk. Following emotionally based impulses is what leads to mediocrity, whereas executing decisions based on need is what increases your chance of rising to the next level.

If you were that homeowner sitting with a house that's overpriced, costing you money, and sucking the life out of your emotional well-being, I'd tell you to accept the bid, take the loss, and move on—not because you want to (I know you don't *want* to, and, frankly, I don't care), but because it's the right business decision and it's what you *need* to do to get yourself focused and back on track.

The Danger of Panicking or Choking

In the middle of the most turbulent market situation we'd seen in more than seventy-five years I got a call from a client named Bruce. "I'm getting killed," he all but shouted into the phone. "Millions of dollars . . . we're losing millions!" Obviously, he was feeling pretty bad. "I'm sorry, man," I told him, "but if you want a hug, call your mom. I don't do pity." Dead silence on the other end. "Listen," I said into the silence. "Don't focus on the losses. What's happened is terrible, but you need to get back in the game. Do you know the opportunities that are out there right now?" More silence. Then he hung up.

I knew I was taking a risk playing hardball with my client, but I also knew I was telling him what he needed to hear—and that is why he hired me in the first place. If I hadn't said what I did, he might have continued to wallow in self-pity and spiral downward. His fund might have gone out of business, and that wouldn't have been good for him, me, or his investors.

Two hours later Bruce called me back. "First," he said, "you are coldhearted. Second, you are right. And thanks for telling me what I needed to hear. Third, I'm done feeling sorry for myself." Then he went on to explain that he'd looked through his portfolio and realized that many of his positions were fundamentally sound and what he needed to do was add to them.

"Are you scared?" I asked. "Hell, yes!" he said. To which I responded, "Good. You *should* be scared. That only means you're human. All that matters is that you avoid panicking or choking."

Everyone gets scared, even the best of the best. In fact, sometimes being scared is the most rational reaction to a given situation. There's no shame in that. It's when people *give in* to those feelings that they get into trouble. As I frequently say to my clients, "Feeling fear is okay so long as you don't act afraid or make a decision because you are afraid."

Allowing fear to get the better of you is a sure road to disaster. Panicking and choking result in different but equally devastating reactions to being in a pressured situation or trying to work in a hostile environment. When you panic, either you develop tunnel vision and can focus on only one thing while you ignore all other pertinent information, or else your mind races around trying to focus on too many things at once so that you can't make logical sense of anything. When you choke, you lose the instinct you would normally have about what to do in a particular situation; you begin to think too mechanically, or you freeze when you need to take action. Either way, your ability to use what you know and to follow your process is temporarily suspended. When that happens, bad decisions (or the negative results of not making any decision) are likely to follow.

Everyone gets scared from time to time. The key is to know when it's happening—there's that self-awareness again that we discussed in Principle #2—and take the steps that will prevent you from making ill-conceived, poorly considered decisions based on hope or fear or both but not on the objective data. Top traders know that any time they find themselves hoping, wishing, or praying, they're about to make a decision based on emotion and they need to stop, step back, and regain their objectivity.

These guys are human, and toxic thoughts do pop into their heads from time to time. But unlike most of us, they don't get overwhelmed and they don't try to fight their thoughts. What they do instead is acknowledge them and then store the thoughts away in a compartment of their brain where they can't influence their decision making. You can do that, too, using the simple strategy I teach my clients. The next time a toxic thought pops into your head, picture yourself putting it in a jar, closing the lid, and putting the jar on your "toxic thought storage shelf," where it will remain out of reach and out of mind.

Panic Attacks and How to Cure Them

I'm assuming that since you're this far along in this book you've already taken the all-important step of getting to know yourself and assessing your strengths and weaknesses so that you will be able to recognize panic when it begins to set in. With that in mind, here's some tried-and-true advice you can use if you find yourself on the brink of joining the Scaredy-cat Club.

First, don't be embarrassed by being afraid, and don't think you need to pretend that you're not. In fact, it would be a good idea to confide in a friend. Tell him that you're afraid you might do something stupid, and enlist his help in holding you accountable for your decisions. (For more on accountability, see Principle #8.) Fear is not bad in itself. In fact, a little fear can sometimes help to put things in perspective and make you more alert. It's only bad when you start making irrational decisions based on the panic you are feeling.

Next, take some time to think through the situation. That doesn't mean procrastinate; it means try to get some clarity. When you're in panic mode, your brain is in fight-or-flight, and you're not really thinking clearly. So stop, count to ten, take four or five long, slow deep breaths, and force yourself to slow down a bit.

Now write out exactly what the worst-case scenario could be. If things were to get as bad as they possibly could, what impact would that have on your life? Seeing the facts laid out in front of you in black and white will likely allow you to see what your emotions have been obscuring. It's unlikely that things are as bad as you've made them seem. Even the riskiest situation is likely to provide some window of opportunity for those who are savvy enough to recognize and take advantage of it.

When circumstances are the most volatile it's those who keep their heads—the Warren Buffetts of the world—who find a way if not to thrive, at least to survive. Remind yourself of the process you've been following and stick to it; do what you *need* to do, not what you *want* to do. There are always aspects of even the scariest situation that are within your control. Take control of what you can instead of letting the situation carry you away.

Remember to think objectively, like a scientist, and stop turning everything into a catastrophe. Use some positive self-talk. As you learned in Principle #3, if you *believe* that something is impossible, it will be. This doesn't mean that if you think positively, everything will always work out or money will be guaranteed to drop into your lap. But it will give you an edge, whereas thinking negatively is sure to tip the odds of success against you.

.   .   .

But, in the end, there's no escaping the fact that life is full of risks. The next principle will help you to get more comfortable with risky situations so that you'll be less likely to panic when people all around you are losing their heads and flailing about in the dark. The most successful traders look at volatility as opportunity, and these days there are plenty of both out there.

PRINCIPLE #7
GET COMFORTABLE WITH
BEING UNCOMFORTABLE

All of our customers with money must someday put it to work—into some revenue-producing investment. Why not invest it now, when securities are cheap? Some people say they want to wait for a clearer view of the future, but when the future is again clear the present bargains will have vanished. In fact, does anyone think that today's prices will prevail once full confidence has been restored? Let us face it—these bargains exist only because of terror and distress. And when the future is assured, the dollar will have long since lost its present borrowing power. It takes courage, of course, to be optimistic about our country's future when nearly everyone is pessimistic. But it is cowardly to assume that the future of the United States is in peril.

—DEAN WITTER, 1932

. . .

Traders know they're operating in a world filled with erratic highs and lows, swings between making and losing money that often occur within the same day. The best ones have learned to be comfortable in that uncomfortable reality.

One of my most successful clients, Carl, runs a $5 billion hedge fund. When one of the most prestigious investment banking and brokerage firms failed in the financial meltdown of 2008, he lost $300 million in one day. Not only was his own net worth seriously affected but also his investors were not very happy. Of course, he wasn't happy either—Carl's human after all. But he also understood that he couldn't control the market, that traders are always making decisions with imperfect information, that he hadn't done anything stupid, he wasn't stealing his clients' money with some elaborate Ponzi scheme, and that even the best performers in this industry are right only about 53 percent of the time.

The difference between Carl and most of the rest of us is that he's learned to be comfortable with the fact that even when he's done all his homework, followed his process, and made responsible investment decisions, there will never be a guarantee that he's made a trade that will make money—because there's no way he can know *everything* there is to know, and some elements will always be beyond his control. Going back to Principle #6, the homeowner couldn't know for certain that the price of his house wouldn't go up, or, if it did, how long that would take; the trader getting rid of a loser couldn't know with absolute certainty that his stock wouldn't rebound. All either one of them could do was collect all the information available at that time, assess the risk/reward ratio, make a decision based on that knowledge, and go to sleep every night knowing that even when he is in the zone and on his game, he might be right only about half the time. Or, as media mogul Rupert Murdoch once said, to be great you have to get comfortable with the knowledge that you are going to make more than twenty important decisions every day, and at least half of those decisions will be wrong. Just like my clients, top performers like Murdoch know that success is a game of probabilities, not perfection.

Living with that kind of uncertainty is what drives most people nuts. It's why so many people get stuck doing nothing or remaining in old, bad habits instead of doing what it takes to change an unpleasant or unprofitable situation.

The Perfect Moment Doesn't Exist

Waiting for that last piece of the jigsaw puzzle or the exact alignment of the stars is what keeps most people tied to a job they hate or afraid to take the step that would get them to the next level in their career. It's what prevents people from breaking free from unhealthy relationships even though they know in their heart of hearts that leaving is the right thing to do. It's not that these people don't want to change; it's just that they keep hoping for some kind of magical moment or mystical revelation that is going to make the final decision for them.

Whenever I talk about the potential consequences of waiting for the perfect moment I think about my maternal grandfather. He was an entrepreneur, an inventor, and a realist. One day he told me the story of how he and my grandmother decided to have a second child. In the midst of World War II, my grandmother was afraid to bring another child into such an uncertain world. When she voiced her fears to my grandfather, he calmly and confidently responded, "My love, that may be the case, but this is the only world we have." Fortunately for me, they decided not to wait for that perfect moment to bring another child into their lives because that second child is my mother.

My grandmother's fears were very real and certainly not unfounded, but more often than not, waiting for the right time to do something results in its never being done at all. I am reminded of a friend who told me that his New Year's resolution was to get in shape and start to eat healthier because his blood pressure and cholesterol levels were "through the roof." I'm sure he expected me to commiserate and praise him for his resolve, but instead I just looked at him as if he were crazy. Why? The reason was because we were having this conversation in the middle of August. I had to ask him what was so magical about January 1? I wasn't trying to be rude or disrespectful; I was really just fascinated. I mean, maybe there was something I simply didn't understand or some secret to which I wasn't privy. Maybe there actually was something special about the calendar's moving from December 31 to January 1 that triggered a transformation in human behavior. As I listened to his "reasons," however, it became clear that what January 1 represented to him was something—anything—he could point to that would allow him not to make his health-improving behavioral changes right now. Today, my friend is alive but still out of shape, so I have to assume that the "perfect moment" never did arrive for him. I can't help wondering whether if he'd actually started his healthier lifestyle program back in August, when he brought it up to me, would he be in better physical shape today? Worse yet, if he continues his unhealthy ways and someday has a heart attack, will he regret not being more proactive about making changes in his life when he had the opportunity to do so?

The lesson is pretty clear. If you want to make a change—I mean, *really* want to make a change—you have to be willing to do it right now. Not later, not tomorrow, not after the weekend, not on January 1, and certainly not only when that eternally elusive perfect moment arrives.

If there were a perfect moment or perfect information, we'd all be making perfect decisions every single time. And, conversely, if we all waited for that perfect moment or until we'd gathered perfect information, no one would ever make any decision at all. The wise among us are those who understand this and use it to their advantage. If you reread the quote at the beginning of this chapter, you'll see that it's exactly what Dean Witter was saying during the Great Depression and it is something that is extremely relevant today.

Learning to Live on the Left Side of Your But

"But" can be one of the most negative words in the English language. How many times have you said (or heard someone else say), "I'd love to quit this job and start my own business, but . . ." or "I wish I could go back to school and get my MBA, but . . ." or any one of the million "buts" with which so many people fill their minds and use to put their lives on hold? All those "buts" are what keep people *sitting on their butts* instead of getting up and doing something to get themselves where they say they really want to be.

Top performers have learned to live on the left side of their "but." They know there will always be "buts," and they understand that they need to keep moving forward in spite of the fact that there will be some risk involved.

Without risk, there's no reward, so the point is to use your edge in order to be sure that the risks you do take are smart risks, and then move ahead knowing that the information you have will never be perfect and that oftentimes a delay results in a missed opportunity. If you can train yourself to think that way, you will come to realize, as my top-performing clients do, that the moment you are in right now is just as perfect, if not more so, for making a decision than any moment in the future. There is never a right time, or, put another way, it is always the right time. Understanding this simple fact is the key to becoming comfortable with being uncomfortable.

Learn to Learn from Your Mistakes

For the average person, having something not turn out the way he had planned might be enough to send him right back to the sofa sitting on his butt. One major difference between the average Joe and the elite performer is the ability to look at disappointments or setbacks as learning opportunities. Perhaps the most often quoted proponent of this productive point of view is Thomas Edison, who after failing ten thousand times to create a safe, practical, and economical incandescent lightbulb was asked why he didn't give up. Edison famously replied, "I have not failed. I've just found ten thousand ways that won't work."

Once again, Tiger Woods comes to mind as an excellent example of the winner who is always willing to use adversity as a means to improve. From 1999 through 2002, Tiger was ranked number one; then in 2003, he fell to number two. In 2004, he won only one major tournament and was ranked fourth. At that point, he stepped back, took a good look at what was going wrong with his game, and reinvented his swing. When asked, Woods said, "People wondered why I made swing changes. You make changes to get better."

In the trading world, you will either make or lose money on any given trade. All that matters in the end is making more money when you're right than you lose when you're wrong. Knowing this, traders have learned to accept failure as part of the game, but they also use the information they acquire from their mistakes as a learning tool. Frequently, what they learn from losing money is more valuable than what they learn when they make money.

As an example of how this works, one of my clients, a guy we'll call Ted, manages a $500 million portfolio trading mainly in the macro markets, meaning the S&P 500 futures, foreign currencies, and commodities such as gold, oil, and natural gas. Ted is constantly monitoring and adjusting his holdings in much the same way a car mechanic listens to an engine and tunes it up as it continues to run. Some of his trades make large profits, while others go against him, forcing him to cut his losses while losing money. Ted doesn't really care which of his holdings are winners and which ones are losers; either way, the market is providing him with a constant stream of information. By paying attention to what's *not* working he becomes better able to focus on what could or should be working and to adjust his positions accordingly. He looks at his portfolio objectively, listens to the engine, so to speak, and continuously fine-tunes it in order to maximize his portfolio's performance.

In the world of retail sales this would mean that the business owner pays close attention to the flow of people through his shop and is aware of which products they're buying or not buying. With this valuable information he can then figure out what's hot and what's not, put the losers on sale, and make sure he keeps the winners in stock.

Use Volatility to Create Opportunity

While others hesitate, winners act. On September 23, 2008, when the news about failing investment banks seemed to be about as bleak as it could get, we got word that Warren Buffett had invested $5 billion in Goldman Sachs—and that was before Congress passed the bailout package that was intended not only to shore up failing financial institutions but also to give investors confidence in the economy's future. Of course, he bought it at what appeared at the time to be a very favorable price, but what gave him the confidence to buy when so many others were selling?

It wasn't that he's worth billions and could "afford" to lose a few, although I'm sure that's what many of you are thinking. If so, I suggest that you think of it in another way. As of the first half of 2008, *Forbes* magazine estimated Buffett's net worth at $62.3 billion. Assuming that figure is accurate (although, given the market conditions since then, it's likely to be significantly lower), investing $5 billion in Goldman Sachs meant that he was taking a risk equal to about 8 percent of his net worth. Putting that into perspective, let's say your net worth (savings and other assets both liquid and nonliquid) is $300,000. Would you have the courage to invest 8 percent of that money, or $24,000, in a Wall Street investment bank right after watching Bear Stearns and Merrill Lynch getting bought out, Lehman Brothers going bankrupt, AIG falling apart, Washington Mutual and Prudential getting gobbled up? Be honest with yourself and you can fully appreciate what Buffett had the courage to do. When all of us—and, yes, I mean all of us—were panicking, calling our financial advisers, and asking if we should sell all of our stocks and go to cash, Warren Buffett, true to form, was looking for opportunity and acting. Is he a genius? No, not really. But he does have a tremendous ability to stay focused during times of panic and to view volatility as a clear and remarkable investment opportunity.

Like all the savviest and most successful investors, Buffett had enough confidence in himself, and enough information about the company he was buying into, to take a very smart risk. He was comfortable enough with being uncomfortable to stay ahead of the crowd, be a leader, and reap the benefits of being decisive when others were wavering.

Uncertainty creates volatility, but people react to it differently. The most successful people don't freeze or panic or buy everything in sight. Instead, they take the time to look around and assess the opportunities available to them. The same opportunities are available to all of us, but only those who have done their homework and who have enough confidence in their own abilities will be able to profit from them while others ponder and pray for perfect information (which does not exist) or wait for overconfirmation (which by then it is too late). If you want the prime cuts of beef you need to be at the head of the line; if you want the icing on the cake you can't wait until there's nothing left but crumbs.

Whatever your personal goal, to be a winner and stay ahead of the pack, you need to get comfortable with uncertainty. I'm not saying you won't be scared. In fact, being scared is sometimes a good thing because it keeps you sharp and on your toes. The key, as I said in Principle #6, is to be scared and still act smart.

Principle #8

Make Yourself

Accountable

He that is good for making excuses is
seldom good for anything else.
—Benjamin Franklin

Go back to Principle #3 and revisit the C.H.A.M.P.® rules I gave you for setting your goals. Probably the single most important rule for successful goal setting is that you need to be accountable for putting your goals into action. Words without action are just philosophy. And, as my old college baseball coach used to tell us, "You can't sit there with the bat on your shoulder and 'look' one out of the park. Sometimes you actually have to swing the bat."

It ought to be perfectly obvious that you can set all the goals you want, but if you don't do anything to achieve them, nothing's going to change. My trading clients may have mapped out the best-constructed investment plan in the world, but if they don't put capital to work and make a trade, they still have zero chance of generating profits. Elite traders live by the credo "Make trades to make money, not to be smart. If you want to be smart, write a book or teach at a university. If you want to make money, you have to put your game plans into action and let the chips fall as they may."

I'm sure most of us set goals with the best of intentions, but because we're all human, more often than not we get distracted, something else comes up, we promise ourselves we'll get to it later, and before we know it another day or a week or a month or a year has gone by and our big plan is still sitting there on the shelf gathering dust while we continue to swear that we're definitely going to get to it . . . soon.

Bridging the Gap Between Wanting and Achieving

I have found that most people honestly and truly do want to change. They want to lose weight or stop smoking or be a more patient parent or a better worker. They really do want to make these changes, not only for themselves but for their families, too. Unfortunately, most people just don't achieve what they want. And the key reasons may be that they lack the structure or discipline or willpower to make change happen. How depressing, and how painful that must be and is for so many.

But why is there such a disconnect between wanting and achieving? Do you remember in Principle #1 that I asked if you wanted to be better at whatever it is you do? My guess is that you responded in the affirmative—or you wouldn't have kept reading. And then, if you recall, I said in Principle #3 that if you wanted to achieve your goal, you needed to commit wholeheartedly to the process and do whatever it took to make it happen. Commitment, perseverance, and discipline are the characteristics that move people beyond desire to action, that differentiate mediocrity from greatness, and that separate greatness from superstardom.

Commitment

My clients have most of the same shortcomings as the average person—in some cases, they even have more. But one thing they do have that is different from most is the willingness to hold themselves accountable—to commit themselves to their goals not because they want to but because they know they have to in order to reach the highest levels of success. Did you ever wonder how Brad Pitt motivated himself to get his body so sculpted for his role as Achilles in *Troy* or how Renée Zellweger got herself to gain twenty pounds for *Bridget Jones's Diary*? Why are some elite athletes willing to follow such rigorous and time-consuming training schedules day after day, year after year? Their desire to be the best at what they do outweighs their desire to *not* do those things.

In the world of sports, swimmer Dara Torres is a prime example of someone who really hates not being the best. Torres has competed, and medaled, in five Olympics, most recently winning three silvers in Beijing at the age of forty-one. To understand just how remarkable an accomplishment that is, consider that when she won five medals in the Sydney games in 2000 at the age of thirty-three, she was the oldest swimmer on the American team. To prepare for Beijing, Torres followed a punishing training routine. In addition to her water workouts, she worked with a strength coach four times a week for sixty to ninety minutes per session as well as a masseuse and a chiropractor who worked on her together for two hours at a time to make her muscles more flexible. Like my clients, she needs to be the best, and she's willing to go to any lengths to achieve her goal.

Perseverance and Leverage

If you have ever completed a marathon you know what it feels like to take yourself to the limit. Now imagine maintaining that intense level of mental toughness each and every day of your life. That is what makes top performers in any field so remarkable. And what I find even more remarkable is that it is a conscious choice they make. But that same choice is also yours to make. The key is to find whatever motivates you and keeps you on track. (Reread Principle #1 if you need reminding.)

Here's how it works. Let's say that you smoke—or pick any self-destructive habit you might have—and you want to stop. You're an intelligent person, you know it's bad for you, you've read all the literature; you know that smoking will probably shorten your life. And yet you continue to do it. Why? I'm sure you have any number of good, justifiable reasons, but the real reason is that you haven't yet found sufficient motivation to quit for good. For you, the pain of quitting—suffering through the symptoms of withdrawal—outweighs whatever the reward might be: in this case, quite possibly a longer and more active life. If I offered you a hundred dollars or even a thousand dollars to quit, that still probably wouldn't change your mind. But what if I told you that if you quit smoking right now, this instant, I'd give you $5 million? The magnitude of that reward would probably outweigh the pain you associate with quitting, and you would definitely find a way to stop. I am confident you would still *want* to smoke, probably every day for the rest of your life. My offer did not change your *want*; instead, what it gave you is a powerful, tangible "why" or motivation to quit. When you heard my offer you would probably tell yourself something like "Wow, never smoking again is going to really suck, but I am sure that, for five million dollars, I will find a way to get over it."

The point is, whatever it is you think you want to change, the reward needs to be great enough to cause you to make a different choice from the one you've been making—even though you still might not *want* to do it. That is called using leverage to modify your current behavior. The most valuable takeaway from this example is that you should never say you "can't" do something. Of course you can; you are just *choosing* not to. But with the right leverage in place and if the risk/reward is shifted sufficiently, you *can* and *will* find a way to achieve what you thought was unachievable and accomplish what you'd believed to be impossible.

Discipline

My trading clients weren't all born with extra genes for discipline. What makes them unique, however, is that they want to be successful so badly that the benefit they will receive from being one of the best traders in the world far outweighs the pleasure they get from being undisciplined.

But what if you can't find a compellingly *positive* reason to change? Then you may need to find your motivation in the unpleasant consequences of *not* changing.

Accountability Requires Consequences

CEOs of public corporations are accountable to their shareholders and to the Securities and Exchange Commission. Politicians who make public statements are accountable to the voters and held accountable because there's a record of what they said. If you borrow money you're accountable to your creditors. And my clients, the mega-wealthy hedge fund managers, are accountable to their investors.

If the CEO fails to make his company profitable or violates the law, he'll be out of a job (and maybe go to jail). If a politician fails to come through on a promise, he faces not only ridicule, embarrassment, and loss of credibility but also potential defeat in the next election. If you use a credit card and don't pay the bill, you'll lose your credit. If you buy a house and don't pay the mortgage, you'll lose your house. If a hedge fund manager doesn't make money for his investors, his investors will withdraw their funds and the hedge fund will go out of business.

But what about those of us who really have no one to answer to but ourselves? Without externally imposed consequences, how do we get motivated and hold ourselves accountable for achieving our goals? For most of us the answer is to enlist the aid of someone to whom we make ourselves answerable.

Why do so many people spend the money to hire a personal trainer instead of working out on their own? Why do some doctors charge patients for missed appointments? Why do businesses conduct employee performance evaluations? Why do professional sports teams fine their athletes if they break team rules? Why do coaches make their players do extra sprints if they show up late to practice? Why does the military threaten soldiers with time in the stockade if they fail to make morning roll call on time? Why have studies shown that college students are more likely to attend classes if they are paying for their own education? In each case it's a way to be held or to hold ourselves accountable through the imposition of an unpleasant consequence.

Knowing that failure to act on a promise we've made to ourselves (that is, a goal we've set) will result in an outcome we'd rather avoid— paying for a service we didn't use or receiving a negative performance evaluation from our supervisor, for example—is a way to make sure we stay motivated, focused, and on target.

Successful traders are willing to do what it takes to keep their edge and stay on top, but they also have enough self-knowledge to be aware that they sometimes need help to be held accountable. That's where I enter the picture. I don't tell these guys how or what to trade. I help them to optimize their thinking and decision-making processes. Similarly, I am not here to tell you how to live your life; I am just helping you to consider some new ways to think about the decisions you make each and every day. And whereas many of us consider that asking for help is a sign of weakness, my clients don't. In fact, they think *not* asking for help is just plain stupid.

Top traders may have reputations for being "masters of the universe" but they know they're not omniscient. They know the markets are bigger than they are, and they're humble enough to know that their job is to listen to what the market is telling them and make objective decisions that will maximize their opportunity to make money. In the end, they know that to think any differently would be ego-driven and a deadly, career-ending mistake.

They also understand that it's easy to be caught up in the stress of the moment and get distracted, so they turn a potential weakness into a strength by asking me to keep them accountable, focused, and on target. Do they like it? Most of the time they don't. But, as I frequently remind them, they are not hiring me to be their friend. They are paying me to push them to become better at what they do. And oftentimes that means telling them what they *need* to hear (*stop letting your emotions determine your actions and listen to what the data are telling you*), not necessarily what they *want* to hear (*it's okay, so don't worry about it, you will do better next time*).

One of the first things I do when I begin to work with a client is to help him determine his weaknesses. (Remember that these guys are already incredibly successful by most people's standards, so there's nothing really to be gained from looking at what they already do well.) For one client the problem might be that he tends to hold on to his losers too long, turning small losses into huge ones; for another it might be that he's too anxious to take his profits, resulting in a higher winning percentage but lower potential profits. Whatever the issue, he, like the habitual smoker, undoubtedly has all kinds of very good reasons for continuing to do what he does even though he knows that he shouldn't be doing it. We could talk about those reasons forever, but that probably wouldn't change a thing. He already knows that the consequence of continuing to do whatever he's doing will be that he makes less money than he should be making, but that obviously isn't sufficient reason for him to change. (Remember, for these guys it is not just about the money.) Therefore, my job is to make sure that the consequence of continuing his bad habit is immediate and painful enough to provide the kind and degree of incentive he needs to change.

To find out what that incentive might be, I ask him: "What do you love? What do you care about? What do you value?" By asking these questions, I am taking him out of the fantasy world of pushing buttons on a screen into the reality of his everyday life. As you can imagine, I've received a variety of very interesting responses. One client told me that he had a Porsche and a Maserati of which he was extremely proud. Growing up he hadn't had very much money and his dream had always been to buy these incredibly expensive, high-performance cars. The consequence I gave him was that the next time he broke one of his own trading rules (which, in his case, was being impatient and putting on trades when he did not have any edge) he'd have to rent a wreck and drive it to work for a week. Conceptually, that idea had such a dramatic impact on his ego that he confessed that the next time he was tempted to break his own rule, a little voice in his head said, "Wait a minute, if you do this you're going to have to drive a piece of junk to work for a week so that everyone will think you're no longer a successful trader." Because that thought was so painful to him, he forced himself to stick to his rules and only make trades when he knew he had a clear edge.

Another of my creative consequences was to tell a client named Richard that the next time he lost money on a trade because he'd done something he knew to be stupid, he would have to sleep in the office. He just stared at me and said, "You mean I'll have to tell my wife I'm not coming home that night? That's crazy. We have two kids and she's six months pregnant with our third one. She'll kill me!" That was exactly the point, and the thought of having to put himself in such an uncomfortable position brought home the potential consequence in a way that was decidedly real.

It may seem illogical to you that something so silly as having to drive a crummy car or having to sleep in the office could have so much more of an effect than the idea of losing hundreds of thousands, if not millions, of dollars. The difference is that those simple consequences are immediate and painful, while, in a way, the money is less real because it is just numbers on a computer screen. In the trading world money comes and goes—appearing and disappearing in a virtual world. No one comes to dump a million dollars on a trader's desk when he makes money or shows up to take it away when he loses on a trade. But he does have to get up and get in that car in the morning; he does have to listen to his wife being angry with him for not coming home.

For another client, the consequence was not being able to eat sushi for a week. I know this doesn't sound like much of a sacrifice, but to him it was because he normally ate sushi *every day.* That was his thing. And for yet another trader, it meant giving his wife five hundred dollars in cash to buy a new pair of shoes each time he made a stupid trade. This was remarkably painful to him because he was appalled by her extravagant shoe habit, which at last count stood at more than 150 pairs at approximately five hundred dollars a pair. (I hasten to explain that those 150 pairs of shoes weren't acquired as a result of 150 stupid things the trader did.)

But I have to caution you to be sure that the consequence you devise for yourself doesn't inadvertently present the opportunity for you to experience it as a reward. So, for example, your consequence shouldn't be that you'll have to donate money to charity, because that would make you feel *good* about yourself and you would also be getting the benefits of a tax deduction. (I did, however, once tell a client, whose office was in Lower Manhattan, that the next time he broke his own rules he'd have to leave his office immediately, go to the bank in the lobby, take six hundred dollars out of the ATM, and throw it in the Hudson River. He had no problem losing $150,000 on a stupid trade, but the idea of throwing away cash from his bank account (even though the amount was substantially less) really got to him. End result: he stuck to his trading rules.

The bottom line is that an effective consequence needs to be something that's going to matter to *you* and have a significant impact on *your* life in a very *immediate* and *meaningful* way. The possibility of losing money on a trade is as ineffective a motivation for a trader as the idea of possibly dying sooner than later is for the habitual smoker.

Change Means Rewards

When my traders make meaningful changes, they're rewarded by making more money and feeling more in control of their emotions and trading decisions. These rewards reinforce their new behaviors, so they are less tempted to break the rules and we don't have to impose consequences nearly as often.

I don't know what's going to cause you enough pain to get you to change, but take a few minutes right now to think of something you've always wanted to achieve but just couldn't make happen. Now, identify something you truly value so that you can use it as leverage to make sure you finally achieve this previously "impossible" task. I am confident that you will find that the task was never impossible. It's just that, until now, the consequence for not doing it was never painful enough. Using leverage is the key to discovering the motivation that works for you.

If you have the self-discipline, you can draw up a contract with yourself, laying out the rules and the consequences for breaking them. Otherwise, you need to find someone who will be your "Dr. Doug" and hold you accountable as I do with my clients. It needs to be someone you trust and someone you respect enough so that you will listen to him when he tells you what you *need* to hear rather than what you *want* to hear—that could be a good friend, a spouse, or a business colleague. The choice—just like the choice to change—is up to you.

Keep a Journal

Another incentive I recommend to help my clients stay on track is keeping a daily performance journal, which is an extremely useful tool for measuring how well you're performing and how much you've progressed toward achieving a goal. I have enhanced this process by having my clients e-mail me the answers to these five simple questions every day.

1. What did I do well today?
2. What did I do poorly?
3. What will I do differently next time?
4. What lessons did I learn?
5. What is my game plan/goal for tomorrow?

This is a relatively painless but extremely insightful process. Weight Watchers, which is arguably one of the most successful diet programs in the world, uses both the weekly weigh-in and journal-keeping to make sure their clients remain accountable.

If you write in your journal on a regular basis, it doesn't take more than ten to fifteen minutes, and those may be the most significant fifteen minutes of your day. Assuming you sleep for eight hours a night, that translates to just 1.5 percent of the time you are awake each day. Do you think it might be worthwhile to invest 1.5 percent of your day in creating positive and meaningful change in your life? If you think you are too busy and just can't find the time to do it, you really need to ask yourself which of the following is going to create the potential for positive and meaningful change in your life: (a) watching fifteen more minutes of TV or surfing the Internet, or (b) investing fifteen minutes to reflect on your goals, successes, and the areas in which you could improve? I think you can answer that by now.

So, what's your excuse for not doing it? Even though most people understand how useful it can be to keep a journal, most won't do it because they'll get sidetracked, get lazy, or use those few minutes to do something else that's more fun and involves less effort. I could ask you how serious you are about taking your game to the next level if you can't find even fifteen minutes in your day to do a quick self-evaluation. But the truth is that many of my clients wouldn't do it either if they didn't make the commitment to e-mail their performance journal to me.

My traders actually thank me for holding them accountable for keeping their journals because they know how important it is. They will admit that it takes very little time once you are in the groove of it. And, what's most important, they experience real and meaningful change in their performance when they do it. Yet it has been my experience that when I don't hold them accountable and don't insist that they send me their journal entries, they stop doing it. That doesn't make sense, does it? After all, they're the ones who say they want to push themselves to the limit and grow to new levels. Ironically, it makes perfect sense because my top-performing clients are still human. They have emotions and fears, distractions and families, and busy lives. But they have to be reminded about their priorities, just like the smoker has to be reminded not to pick up that cigarette or the dieter not to pick up that chocolate brownie.

So, if you have a mind to keep a daily performance journal, you may just want to find your own "Dr. Doug" to whom you can e-mail your entries. There's no need to burden someone with the responsibility of reading and commenting on these pages. Just ask your "Dr. Doug" to acknowledge their receipt—and to remind you when you failed to send them. Your own "coach" might also be willing to help you come up with a real and meaningful consequence for your failure to do what you said you were going to.

By making this commitment to another person whose opinion you value, you will be more likely to follow through on your commitment to yourself. And if that doesn't do the trick, it doesn't mean you're destined for failure; it simply means you need to raise the reward or consequence bar a bit to really force yourself into changing your behaviors.

How Motivated Are You?

I'm sure there are some readers who'll say, "Oh, I don't need to be accountable to anyone else. I have enough willpower—and I want this badly enough to be accountable to myself." If so, that's great. Good for you! But you should understand that when push comes to shove, even the most self-motivated among us may need a little extra incentive to keep us going. And, I repeat, there's no shame in asking for help—so long as you fess up to yourself and take the necessary steps to counteract what is, after all, no more than your natural human tendency to get distracted or despondent or lazy.

Question: If you smoke and you decide to quit, which of the following is better?

1. Use the patch.
2. Chew a nicotine-substitute gum product.
3. Quit cold turkey all on your own.

Answer: Your goal is to quit smoking; there are no bonus points for doing it a certain way, and if you think otherwise, your ego is getting in the way. You just need to do whatever it takes to stop. Unfortunately, most people believe that doing it on their own, without help, makes them better or more worthy. That simply isn't true. In the end, it's all about what works for you. I can show you the tools and share the principles behind my 8 Ways to Great, but I can't force you to implement them. The real path to joining the ranks of the elite is this: you've got to want it enough to be willing to do whatever it takes to make it happen.

So, now that you know what it takes, what are you going to do?

For more information about Dr. Doug Hirschhorn,
his blog, products, and coaching services, please visit
www.DrDoug.com

THE 8 PRINCIPLES
AT A GLANCE

Principle #1: Find Your "Why?"

Determine your core motivation. Once you know why you do what you do, why you want to do it better, or why you want to do something else, you'll have put the key in the engine that's going to drive you to figure out how to achieve your vision.

Principle #2: Get to Know Yourself

Gaining a new perspective on your strengths and weaknesses allows you to concentrate on and leverage what you do best at the same time you minimize the chances of being held back by your weaknesses.

Principle #3: Learn to Love the Process

In order to reach your ultimate goal or vision, you need to have a plan—a series of short-term goals whose achievement is within your control. Following these steps will become your process. The process is what keeps you focused on the here and now, on what you need to do in the moment to move on to the next level.

Principle #4: Sharpen Your Edge

There are two sides to your edge: The first is determining and using whatever it is that sets you apart from other people in your field to give you an advantage. The second is finding out as much as you can about the odds and the potential payoff before you make any decision, even if it means making decisions with imperfect information. If you do that, things may not always go according to plan, but you will not be guilty of taking thoughtless risks or making stupid mistakes.

Principle #5: Be All That *You* Can Be

Judge yourself only in terms of your own abilities. Always strive for your personal best. Don't be limited by comparing yourself to others and aiming only to be as good as or better than the next guy.

Principle #6: Keep Your Cool

It's okay (even human) to be scared, but it's not okay to act out of panic. Do what's needed in every situation even though your ego, emotions, or the need to be right may be telling you to do something different. Be aware that what you want may be different from what's best for you and/or your business.

Principle #7: Get Comfortable with Being Uncomfortable

The most successful people know that there is never a perfect moment to make a decision and that they will never have the perfect information they seek. They understand that he who hesitates runs the risk of missing out on an opportunity while someone else seizes the moment to profit from his indecision. Top traders have learned to be comfortable acting upon imperfect information, to be decisive while the rest of the world continues to deliberate, and to use their own and other people's mistakes as opportunities to learn and improve.

Principle #8: Make Yourself Accountable

Be accountable—to yourself, your goals, and to others. Unless there is some meaningful reward for performing well and an equally meaningful consequence for making a stupid mistake or breaking your own rules, you may not take the steps necessary to put your best-laid plans into action. If you feel you don't have the discipline to hold yourself accountable, find someone you trust who will hold your feet to the fire.

ACKNOWLEDGMENTS

I have always believed that ideas without action are just philosophy. While the ideas in this book are drawn from my unique expertise and experiences as a peak performance coach to the Wall Street elite, there are many people who helped me put them into action. I am grateful to each and every one of you for seeing to it that so many people will now be able to benefit from these lessons and insights.

First and foremost, my dear friend and mentor Robbie Vorhaus: You are a blessing and a gift. Thank you, my brother, for reminding me that all is well.

To my agent, Kate Lee: Thank you for meeting with me, hearing what I had to say, understanding the value of my idea, and agreeing on the spot to represent me.

To my editor and publisher, John Duff: Thank you for seeing the potential in this book. You really went above and beyond in your commitment to helping me articulate the core concepts. Working with you has been a truly enjoyable experience that I hope we'll repeat in the future.

To Judy Kern: Thank you. You are a rock star.

ACKNOWLEDGMENTS

To all my clients: Thank you all for allowing me to tell you what you need to hear rather than what you want to hear. And last, but not least, to my three incredible children, Sam, Charlie, and Ryan: Thank you for reminding me every day about what is truly important in life.